A Preachable

A Preachable Message

St. John Chrysostom, patron saint of preachers

Cover art by Diana and George Voyajolu
St. John Chrysostom, born in Antioch, c. 347 to 407

Considered the most prominent doctor of the Greek Church and the greatest preacher ever heard in a Christian pulpit, St. John Chrysostom is often referred to as "golden-mouthed" because of his eloquence.

It has been written that he ordinarily preferred moral subjects. The frequent outbursts of applause during his homilies undoubtedly inspired him to forge ahead.

Ordained a priest in 386, John was given the chief task of preaching for the next twelve years. After the bishop of Constantinople died on September 27, 397, John Chrysostom was ordained bishop to take his place. The story goes that he began "sweeping the stairs from the top." In his own household, he put an end to the lavish living of his predecessor and lived simply. He built a large hospital with the money he had saved in his household during the first year.

For much more of the interesting life of St. John Chrysostom, please visit www.newadvent.org.

ISBN: 0-9722251-0-2

Printed in the United States of America
by Versa Press, Inc., East Peoria, Illinois.

Published by
The Billings Ovulation Method Association - U.S.A.
P.O. Box 16206
St. Paul, Minnesota 55116
651-699-8139
e-mail: boma-usa@msn.com
www.boma-usa.org

Dedication

This book is dedicated to

Pope John Paul, II, for his timeless wisdom and inspirational writings. We will be forever grateful to God for him.

Most Reverend George H. Speltz, retired bishop of the Diocese of Saint Cloud, Minnesota, who saw the value and need of Natural Family Planning at a time when *Humanae Vitae* was not received with wholehearted enthusiasm and support. His concern for the Christian family was an integral part of his tenure as bishop of Saint Cloud.

Drs. John and Evelyn Billings, Melbourne, Australia, who pioneered the development of modern Natural Family Planning. Their fifty years of devotion to science and methodology has benefited couples worldwide. It is with deep gratitude that we acknowledge their gifts to humanity.

Acknowledgments

We are deeply grateful to the many contributors to this publication who have demonstrated their support and promotion of the Church's teaching contained in *Humanae Vitae*. We offer our thanks and salute their courage and steadfastness to this most important apostolate.

It is with heartfelt thanks that we acknowledge the distinguished editing skills and expertise of Father Thomas Knoblach, as he cheerfully assisted with this publication. We also recognize and offer sincere appreciation to Peg Conroy for her meticulous initial transcription of the audio tape and to Missy Ohmann for her patience, understanding, and assistance with this project, which has been invaluable. Without any of these people, this work would not have come to fruition.

TABLE OF CONTENTS

Foreword

During the summer of 1998, I worked for Father Daniel McCaffrey, S.T.D., at his NFP Outreach office in Oklahoma City. We would have long and interesting discussions on why Natural Family Planning, *Humanae Vitae*, and contraception were not being broached from the pulpit by the clergy.

This 100-percent Irish, New York City born and bred priest would pound his fist on the table with each word, saying, "Sue, THIS IS A PREACHABLE MESSAGE!"

But why wasn't it being preached more often?

Giving the benefit of doubt, I surmised that, in many cases, this was simply because many priests and deacons were not sure what to say or how to say it. Hence, the idea for an audiotape was born. I put out a plea to colleagues in the field of Natural Family Planning to send me the names of clergy who they knew had spoken from the pulpit on this watershed topic. ("From the pulpit" was key to deciding which cardinal, bishop, priest, or deacon would be interviewed.) Names came pouring in from all parts of the United States.

Recorded either in person or by telephone, these clergy were asked to talk about their personal experience discussing this counter-cultural issue from the pulpit. Consistently, they found the feedback from the people in the pews to be positive and affirming.

The tape, "NFP: A Preachable Message," has received widespread acclaim. Thanks to publicity from such widely read publications as the *National Catholic Register*, the tape has been ordered by people from all over the United States and as far away as Notre Dame Cathedral in Paris, France. Some dioceses have purchased a tape for each priest, deacon, and seminarian.

Early in its distribution, we were asked if the tape was available in printed form. Priests asked for sample homilies. *Voila!* The need for this book became clear.

So, it is with grateful thanks to the Saint Cloud Diocesan Office of Natural Family Planning, in particular Kay Ek, the director, who supported this important project since its inception, that I am able to tell you how this simple idea has made its way into the hands and hearts of our spiritual leaders.

As Francis Cardinal George says in his introduction, "It is my prayer that by listening to their personal testimonies the Holy Spirit will guide you to a new zeal and a new commitment to promoting the truth."

Sue Ek, Executive Director
Billings Ovulation Method Association - USA

THE FIRST SECTION OF THIS BOOK CONSISTS OF EMENDATIONS OF INTERVIEWS FOUND ON THE AUDIO TAPE, *NFP: A PREACHABLE MESSAGE*. THEY APPEAR IN THE ORDER AS THEY DO ON THE AUDIO TAPE. THE TEXTS THAT FOLLOW ARE EXAMPLES OF HOMILIES THAT ADDRESS THE THEMES OF *HUMANAE VITAE*.

INTRODUCTION

Dear brothers in Christ,

We all know that perhaps one of the most difficult issues to address, not only from the pulpit but even in person,

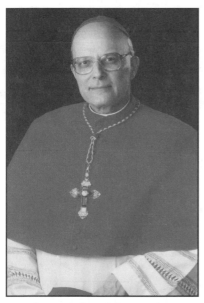

His Eminence Francis Cardinal George, OMI, Archdiocese of Chicago, Illinois.

is the Church's teaching on contraception and Natural Family Planning. Yet in my pastoral experience, the mutual respect that grows between husband and wife using Natural Family Planning is beautiful to see and fruitful for the Church. The Catholic clergy who share their reflections with you here have all preached the beauty of Natural Family Planning and *Humanae Vitae* from the pulpit. It is my prayer that by listening to their personal testimonies the Holy Spirit will guide you to a new zeal and a new commitment to promoting the truth. Natural Family Planning is a preachable message because it is a gospel message, always keeping together love and life.

Father James Sullivan, OP

My overwhelming experience in preaching about contraception is that it is a message that people have readily received, not only in marriage preparation, but also in terms of married couples who struggle with the question of how many children the Lord is calling them to have and wanting to be faithful to His plan. I not only present the clear teaching of the Church to couples, but I also encourage them to investigate Natural Family Planning as a real means for being faithful to each other, being open to life and growing in their Catholic faith.

Father James Sullivan, O.P.
Teacher of Theology at Saint Joseph's
Seminary Dunwoodie, Yonkers, New York

My experiences have really reminded me of the great import of truth in people's lives. They come to realize that when the Church teaches something, she does not teach it as if she made it up, but rather because the teaching is true in and of itself. Such truth then resonates with the believer's heart and mind.

This truth especially reveals the lie of contraception. If a couple is trapped in contraception, they realize this. Thus, when they hear the truth of the Church's moral teaching, they are naturally drawn to it—even if it may be difficult—and even if they might struggle with it, and even if they might be mad or angry that they are caught in something contrary to it. But ulti-

4

mately it will only be truth that will set them free; it will only be truth that can help them to love each other as husband and wife. And it will only be truth that will make them happy with themselves, with their relationship with the Lord, with their married love for each other, and with their family.

So, to those who are struggling with questions like, "How do I preach about Natural Family Planning? How do I preach about contraception?" I say: have no fear, preach the truth in love, and truth and love together will make converts and disciples of all nations.

Deacon Doctor Bob McDonald

Deacon Dr. Bob McDonald, Diocese of Pembroke, Ontario. Permanent Deacon, Medical Doctor, Practice of Psychotherapy, Barry's Bay, Ontario, Canada.

I have been a medical doctor since 1963 when I graduated from Edinburgh University in Scotland. I have taught at the university as an assistant professor of family medicine, teaching psychotherapy. When I ended that part of my career, I moved very smoothly into the practice of psychotherapy full time. I bill myself as a Catholic psychotherapist, so that most of my work involves a great deal of spiritual direction as well as the professional side of psychotherapy itself.

In addition to these roles, I am also a permanent deacon in the Roman Catholic Church. I have been preaching on contraception from the pulpit in my parish for well over a decade. At every opportunity, I mention the damaging effects of contraception on the relationship of husband and wife. I also discuss the abortifacient probability of the contraceptive pill.

At the same time, I also try to have people understand that the Church's concern with contraception is not just about the birth control pill; there is a whole variety of techniques which violate our own dignity and the rights of God in our marriage covenant. That covenant is between husband and wife, yes; but that is not the whole picture. The marriage covenant is in fact between husband, wife, and God. It is indeed a Trinitarian experience "till death do us part."

My parishioners express appreciation of this preaching. The comment that I hear most frequently is, "Why weren't we told this before? We never heard it, we needed to hear it, and we are so glad that you are standing up and being counted and telling us what the truth is." I encourage those who preach to just stand up and say what needs to be said. Ask the Holy Spirit to guide your words and to open the hearts of your people. It is true that there will be some opposition from one or two individuals. But quite frankly, it is worth it for the kingdom of God.

Archbishop Charles Chaput, O.F.M., Cap.

One of the things that constantly surprises me—I would even say astonishes me—is the number of people who come to talk to me after I have preached about *Humanae Vitae*. Whether

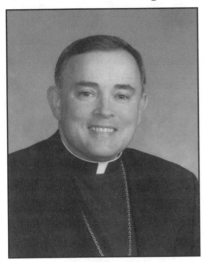

Archbishop Charles Chaput, O.F.M., Cap.
Archdiocese of Denver, Colorado

I speak about this teaching directly or as an example within another topic, many come and say how grateful they are that I had the courage to speak about contraception. Almost always, I simply respond that it doesn't really take any particular courage because to speak the truth of Christ without compromise is really part of the essential ministry of a bishop or a priest.

In the course of thirty-one years of priestly ministry, I have seldom experienced any negative reaction to preaching about *Humanae Vitae* and about the importance of Natural Family Planning for happy marriages and family life. I believe it is very important for our priests not to be afraid. They will find that the Lord gives them the strength to communicate this teaching in the right way, to speak it clearly. And I believe they will be astonished at the response that such preaching generates in the lives of the faithful.

Father John Corapi, S.T.D., S.O.L.T

My name is Father John Corapi. Why should the clergy preach *Humanae Vitae*? For the simple reason that it is the teaching of the Church. It is an encyclical, an encyclical that binds in conscience. It teaches us what the Church has always taught—that human life is sacred. This is not optional teaching; it is essential teaching. Artificial contraception is intrinsically evil. Is it possible for a Catholic in good conscience to take birth control pills or engage in other forms of artificial contraception? The simple answer is a resounding no. Very often we are not hearing this message from the pulpit because it is not politically correct in what has been rightly termed "a culture of death." "The Church should stay out of the bedroom," some say. The Church rightly goes where she

Father John Corapi, S.T.D., S.O.L.T,
Diocese of Sacramento, California

needs to go in order to form consciences and teach truth. If the Church fails to teach and preach this essential message, then she should rightly consider herself guilty of failing in her pastoral responsibility. Every Catholic should read this courageous and timely encyclical of Pope Paul VI. One might ask if Catholics are really interested in this, do they still seek the truth? I have preached in forty-nine states and all of the Canadian provinces except one, plus several foreign countries. I can tell you that

8

Catholics, and others too, love the truth, seek the truth, and most of all - deserve the truth. It is our sacred duty as bishops and priests, and the laity for that matter, to teach and preach the eternal truth contained in Pope Paul VI's great Encyclical *Humanae Vitae*.

Father Kenneth Baker, S.J.

Father Kenneth Baker, S.J., editor of the *Homiletic and Pastoral Review,*

I am the editor of the *Homiletic and Pastoral Review,* which is a monthly magazine for the Catholic clergy. Over the last twenty-seven years, I've published several articles about Natural Family Planning. I have also preached about *Humanae Vitae* several times. This preaching has been very well received.

Pope Paul VI in *Humanae Vitae* was very prophetic when he predicted what would happen in a culture that becomes a contraceptive society. There are many people talking about the decline of American culture because of the aberrations in the whole sexual area; Paul VI predicted that. What he foresaw is exactly what has come about.

Archbishop Harry J. Flynn

Our Holy Father, Pope Paul VI, gave the Church this beautiful gift in 1968, the encyclical *Humanae Vitae*. We all remember the response to that gift. In many corners of the Church, it was negatively received. However, there were also many others who looked upon it as a document that would be acclaimed as one of the great lights of our century, a century known for a great deal of violence and darkness and even a certain atmosphere of death.

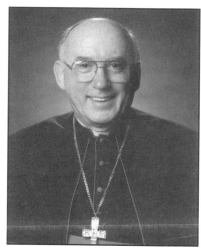

Archbishop Harry Flynn
Archdiocese of Saint Paul-Minneapolis,
Minnesota

Humanae Vitae is a beautiful document that speaks about human life, human love, and the final destiny that we all have in God's life and love. For many years, we have been diffident in preaching this very beautiful truth, and I think the diffidence arises because of a certain human respect. We realize that many people would still be in disagreement with the truth of *Humanae Vitae*. However, from my own experience, whenever I have preached on a difficult subject in a pastoral way, preaching from the beauty of the truth which the Church presents to us, my message has been more than well received.

We always need to be pastoral, as *Humanae Vitae* demonstrates so well. But we also need to have the courage to preach God's Word without fear. We must preach it from our own experience, with hope that the words that we use will be filled with grace and help people to be what God wants them to be.

Father Ronald Lawler, O.F.M., Cap.

I work in the Diocese of Pittsburgh with family and adult religious education and in Natural Family Planning and marriage preparation. I see more and more that Natural Family Planning is the core of a response to an immense need in the Church, and the source of infinite blessings.

Father Ronald Lawler, O.F.M., Cap. Director of Religious Education—Adults and Families, Diocese of Pittsburgh, Pennsylvania, author of **Teaching of Christ** and other works

The Church has always known that marriage has to be a vocation to holiness and that marriages require generosity, a certain greatness of heart. However, the world tries to teach us—as Catholics and others who believe in Christ—ways of thinking about sexuality, marriage, and love that just don't work.

We can see from experience that some marriages and homes work, and some don't. When we look at this experience more closely, we see that

11

those who are following wise and good ways of respecting sexuality and the partners' identities come to understand the wisdom behind God's plan. They find that being generous works for their marriages. This generosity is not painful; it is a response to God's call. These generous marriages last, and the spouses have an awareness of how good God is to them in their lives. They see that God wants them to do things that are healthy for love, for marriage, for little children, for all the most important things in the world.

The Holy Father is constantly talking of the importance of teaching people about Natural Family Planning. Mother Teresa of Calcutta did. Many holy people in the Church have realized that marriages have to be lived in the faith and in the generosity that Christ teaches. Priests have to be aware that there is nothing to fear in speaking of this. Of course, we can teach *anything* in the faith stupidly and badly and in ways that hurt. But *this* element of chaste, pure and generous love can be taught without great difficulty. People can understand that priests are trying to teach something that they need and that they really want.

Bishop Thomas J. Olmsted

Every year on the Sunday nearest to July 25 (the anniversary of *Humanae Vitae*), I always preach on *Humanae Vitae* and Natural Family Planning. It is such an important part of our teaching that the anniversary is a good time for me to

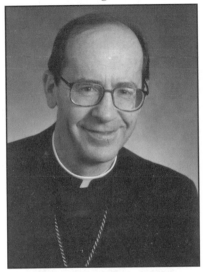

make sure that at least once a year I address these issues. I also look for opportunities to fit it easily and appropriately into homilies and talks I give.

What has been the result of my preaching? Well, I know that couples who practice Natural Family Planning are encouraged; they're very grateful, and they feel strengthened to continue. And teachers and doctors and priests and others also find encouragement when someone comes forward and supports the Church's teaching.

Bishop Thomas Olmsted, D.D.
Diocese of Wichita, Kansas

More importantly, every time that I preach on Natural Family Planning and the Church's teaching in the area of sexuality, I myself grow in my own trust of the truth. I become more confident in my ability to speak about varied facets of married life, not only Natural Family Planning, but other aspects as well. If I were to have a doubt about the Church's teaching that would cause me to be silent about any part of it, such doubt would tend to undercut my confidence in other areas. However, if I really make the effort to preach about what are the

13

more difficult parts for some people, my own effort to do so deepens my own trust in the truth, and makes me more grateful for the Church's teaching in this regard. So I would strongly encourage my brother priests and bishops to take opportunities to teach and to explain and persuade others to the goodness of the Church's teaching on sexuality and, in particular, Natural Family Planning.

Father Alan Okon

I gave a homily on Respect Life Sunday last year that had surprising results. As I approached the pulpit, I did not necessarily have the intention of preaching on respect for life; however, I was moved by the Holy Spirit at that point in time. In a nutshell, I spoke about how the current culture of death is connected with the contraceptive movement from the 1950s, which moved into abortion, and is moving into euthanasia. I spoke about our responsibility to transform this culture of death into a culture of life, and I gave some examples on how that has happened.

Unbeknownst to me, there was an OB/GYN attend-

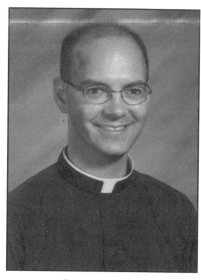

Father Alan Okon
Parochial Vicar, Archdiocese, Philadelphia, Pennsylvania

14

ing that Mass who had been working with another priest as he considered changing his practice to a specifically Natural Family Planning practice. A few weeks later, it came to my attention that, because of my homily and the manner in which it was preached with the Holy Spirit working, this doctor had a conversion experience. As a result of a number of things coming together, he has gone with an NFP-only practice.

Our parish sees NFP as being very important for our community life as a whole. Another priest here had worked with Natural Family Planning in the archdiocese and was involved here in adult catechesis. We see Natural Family Planning as an important component of our marriage preparation course. So when we sit down with our couples one-on-one, it is most certainly a topic that we discuss. Our pre-Cana teams also explain to couples the reasons to use NFP, both from a moral perspective and also from a biological perspective.

NFP has a lot of both physical and spiritual benefits, trusting in the Lord and allowing God to continue to work within our lives. We believe that God, who has called us to this point in life, is not going to abandon us but still works within our lives. He will never call us to something that we are unable to handle.

Father Anthony Oelrich

The Church is called to proclaim good news. I think one of the most beautiful expressions of the good news that the Church can proclaim to this age is deeply connected with its teaching on Natural Family Planning and against contraception. For the Catholic Church to proclaim good news is always to proclaim a very concrete living reality, not something that is far away or far off, but something that is very much a part of our lives; Jesus came to affect our lives. There's a constant temptation on the part of priests, I think, to make the proclamation of the Gospel

Father Anthony Oelrich
Priest of the Diocese of St. Cloud,
Minnesota, studying in Rome, Italy.

something perhaps a little abstract; because when it becomes concrete then it impinges on our lives and it demands change.

People are in need of the good news, and in our culture marriage is in need of good news. There is so much stress on marriage. When I deal with young people, I often sense a kind of hopelessness or anxiety or fear: "Can I make a lifetime commitment?"

The Church's teaching on Natural Family Planning really says one can do this: one can live in a beautiful relationship of love that really images God's love for His people. It further presents a concrete way, in the practice of Natural Family Planning, to bring that love alive in one's married life. To proclaim it is part of proclaiming the Gospel, the good news that

Jesus calls us to in so many ways throughout the Gospels that we read Sunday by Sunday.

Father Daniel McCaffrey

I go through the country week after week speaking in parishes about Natural Family Planning and the moral imperatives that underlie it regarding contraception and sterilization. And I affirm without any ambiguity, that this is a very, very preachable message.

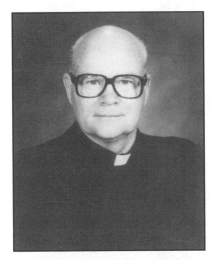

Father Daniel McCaffrey, STD
Director, Natural Family Planning
Outreach, Oklahoma City, Oklahoma

I remember very distinctly that when *Humanae Vitae* came out over thirty years ago, Pope Paul VI addressed himself to priests in a special way. He begged the priests to preach this message and not to be afraid to preach it. The Holy Spirit that animates the teaching office of the Church and its preaching is the same Spirit that is in the hearts of our good people who listen to the message; therefore, it resonates within them.

I can say from experience that there is no question about it; when this message, this good news of Natural Family Planning, and the good news of God's message and the Ten Commandments are preached to the people in their entirety, the people do listen. Our people do deserve to hear these messages; they have every right to hear them. And when they do hear the message of Natural Family Planning, their lives blossom; vocations come about in the Church, marriages are enhanced, communication is increased between the couples. This preaching has a great benefit and a great value. As a pastor, I know from many years of experience that this is a very, very preachable message.

Monsignor Bob Guste

I am in the full-time ministry of giving missions and retreats, and using the media and doing some writing for the purpose of evangelization. Years ago, as a younger priest—I've been a priest for about fifty years—I was not wholeheartedly in support of the Church's position against contraception. The turning point was when I attended a conference in which I heard, for the first time in my life, that the pill together with all the other chemical contraceptives—Depo-Provera, Norplant and so on—have an abortive potential. That's not just some of them, but all of them, all of the pills included. That shocked me.

Monsignor Bob Guste
Ministry of Evangelization and Spiritual Renewal

18

And in this particular presentation the other harmful side effects of the chemical contraceptives were also presented. For example, the package insert in a package of pills lists countless possible side effects. The former president of Pharmacists for Life told me that he hasn't met one person who has not experienced some bad effect from them. Those facts, together with the good effects of Natural Family Planning, were for me like a light going on, saying, "Hey, there's something wrong with contraception! There's something right about Natural Family Planning."

But the biological facts are not the main reason, of course, why contraception is wrong. It is wrong because in sharing with us the power to give life, God joined it to an intimate expression of self-giving love. To unnaturally separate the act of love from its possible life-giving effect is to tamper with and seriously violate the sacred gift of God. It is similar to the words of Jesus, "What God has joined together let no man put asunder." We don't have the right to do that.

What I see in my ministry is that once people begin to start making up their minds as to just what they want to do in this regard, then they make up their minds about all kinds of other things—in sexual morality, in morality in general, and in regard to doctrinal matters—even such a sacred reality of our faith as the Holy Eucharist.

Before 1930 all Christians stood shoulder to shoulder on this issue. It was in 1930 that the Anglican church at their Lambeth conference began to reluctantly make some exceptions regarding contraception. Then so many denominations began to collapse on the issue. We need to get back once again to following the Church, knowing that God sent His Son as "the light of the world" and the Son established His Church. Clearly, "As the Father has sent me," He said, "so I send you."

And we need to start listening once again to the Church for the direction that we need.

Father James Otto

I was ordained a priest in May of 1997 here in the Archdiocese of Philadelphia, and I find that Natural Family Planning is definitely a preachable message. I present it in the context of the question, "Why does the Church say 'no' to contraception and sterilization, but 'yes' for a just reason to Natural Family Planning?"

I've been preaching and teaching this in a number of ways. The most fertile ground has really been in marriage preparation, and I've done a lot of work with our pre-Cana group and working one-on-one with couples in marriage preparation. Spending time with couples, I find them very open and receptive. People will say couples can't be forced to use Natural Family Planning. While that is true, if one does not present the full teaching, the culture will force them into contraception and sterilization. I find couples to be very thankful for this knowledge.

Father James Otto
Priest of the Archdiocese of Philadelphia, Pennsylvania

20

When couples come to marriage preparation, initially they're probably thinking a lot more about sex than about God. Giving them God's vision, the Church's vision of marriage, family and sexuality, has really been a tool to draw them into a relationship with the Lord and the Church.

I have also preached this message from the pulpit. I have focused upon the fact that there is a very strong link between contraception and abortion. In response, people have been grateful: "Father, we haven't heard this; thank you for giving us the truth." For me, it has been a very rewarding and fruitful part of my priesthood.

I would encourage my brother priests to follow in the footsteps of Pope John Paul II. The doctrine underlying *Humanae Vitae* has definitely been a major part of his pontificate, reflected in his theology of the body. He really gives a very convincing apologetic for the teaching.

Bishop Frederick Campbell

I am grateful for this opportunity to speak about Natural Family Planning and about the wonderful vision that our Holy Father Pope Paul VI painted for us in his encyclical *Humanae Vitae*. I have come to realize what a positive contribution NFP can make to marriages, and through those marriages to the lives of our parishes. I have found that people who have discovered the great gift of NFP have firmer marriages, stronger family life, and are wonderful contributors to the life of their whole parish.

Bishop Frederick Campbell
Auxilary bishop, Archdiocese of St. Paul-Minneapolis, Minnesota

I have always encouraged Natural Family Planning. I see its great strength, especially in our present situation in a kind of cultural breakdown of marriage, which, as Pope Paul VI predicted, would derive from the widespread use of contraception. So I encourage couples to investigate Natural Family Planning. I know many people who are trained in its presentation, and I know many who are practicing it. All are witnesses to the wonderful gift that it is to the Church.

Father Bob Cannon

I find John Paul II's reflections on human sexuality to be beautiful and very, very rich. I have also found the same teaching about human sexuality to be very applicable to couples, to those who are engaged, and to young people. Specifically, when I'm talking to any of these groups—whether it's in the celebration of the Eucharist, with marriage en-

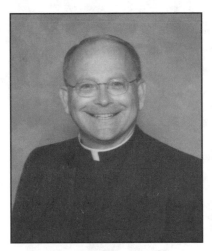

Father Robert Cannon, JCL
Priest of the Diocese of Venice, Florida,
Judical Vicar, Rector of Epiphany Cathedral

counter groups, or with couples one on one—I point out how Christianity, and especially Catholicism, is a bodily religion. It is meant to be incarnational; every one of us is called to embody God's love. It is our vision of human sexuality that through our bodies we become the sacraments, so to speak, by which we touch the world. Thus, how we use our bodies is vitally important when we talk about our relationships, not only with God, but also with one another.

I ask couples, "What do you think it is that makes marriage holy?" Sometimes people say, "Well, it's because the marriage occurred in the church, or it's a sacrament," and things like that. I say, "No, no, no. What really makes marriage holy?" And then I will draw out from them that when people love generously and totally and unconditionally, then that kind of love invites God's presence; God blesses this love and calls it sacred.

So we can truly call marriage a holy bond. When a couple loves generously and cooperates entirely with the stewardship of their fertility in NFP, then all of their love-making becomes body-prayer.

And as soon as they start realizing that their fecundity, their passion, their loving embrace is all wrapped up in that vocation to embody God's love, they look at how they express their love and affection with new eyes, with a whole new vision. Then they can make the connection that contraception brings things into their body-prayer contrary to embodying God's love. One need not go into a lot of detail about contraceptive methods. With just these general principles people will be able to filter out what is good and holy and what is not.

Father William Kurz, S.J.

I have been teaching at Marquette University for twenty-nine years. I have been involved more intensely with Natural Family Planning the last several years.

As a teacher, I've found a lot of prejudice to overcome in trying to talk to students about contraception and human sexuality. I've had to overcome the effects of the sexual revolution, to which they have all been exposed. I tried to point out the sufferings that result from that revolution, especially the broken families, the diseases, the heartbreaks, and on and on. With that approach, the students could listen and understand and at least hear what I was trying to say.

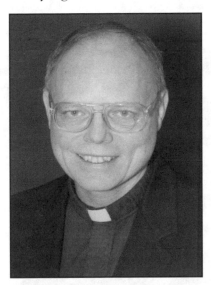

Father William Kurz, S.J.
Professor of Theology, Marquette University, Milwaukee, Wisconsin

When I am either preaching or teaching, I try to talk about how in the '60s or the '70s, when the Pill came in, people were so arrogant, even about how we could manipulate nature with technology. In the '80s and '90s, we have come to see how this manipulation has caused a good deal of ecological pollution, and that one must respect nature. I try to stress that NFP shows respect for women as women, and for what people would be most distressed about if it were lost: their fertility.

It is a struggle to get people to listen, but we have the truth—a beautiful truth. This is a truth that deals with women's health and not just Church teachings. I do not stress Church teaching as such; I stress the intrinsic values of NFP. Of course, I do then talk about *Humanae Vitae*, which I consider one of the most beautiful, insightful and powerful documents.

Father Joseph Hattie

I have had the opportunity on a number of occasions to preach on *Humanae Vitae* and Natural Family Planning. I have found a very positive response to this teaching; couples do, in the great majority of cases, want to hear more. They want to be able to understand the truth that can set them free in living their own vocation more fully and more faithfully to themselves, to God, and to their family and to the Church.

I would encourage all the clergy to take advantage of the opportunities they may have to preach on this very, very important topic, which is so essential for our age and our time. Our era denies the gift of fertility, and it, therefore, tries to influence couples to this

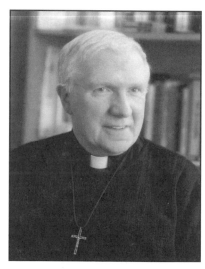

Father Joseph Hatti, OMI
Consultant, Archdiocese of Halifax,
Nova Scotia, Canada

same view. It leads into the culture of death, instead of into the culture of life in which they would put their fertility at the service of life and the service of the salvation of others as our Blessed Mother has herself done.

Father Pablo Straub, C.S.S.R.

Priests and bishops are not allowed to be selective in staying with the Church, that is to say, in the preaching of the Gospel. We can no more set aside *Humanae Vitae,* in its solemn teaching concerning what marriage is for and, therefore, what the marriage act is for, than we can be silent about the Real Presence or Mary's virginity or the Most Holy Trinity.

Father Pablo Straub, C.S.S.R.
Redemptorist Missionary

Now, what is *the* thing in our day that interferes with the flow of sacramental grace in marriage, and threatens to block out its effects? I am convinced it is artificial contraception. And so it becomes our duty to explain the evil inherent in this sin of our day. Contraception probably is the root sin of our day, since out of the mentality of contraception spring other more horrid sins, such as abortion.

Natural Family Planning is certainly helpful to couples. In a society where divorce is creeping towards fifty percent, practitioners of Natural Family Planning, including agnostics, have a divorce rate somewhat below five percent. That tells us something about how NFP humanizes married life and helps couples naturally. And NFP is practicable. The fact that so many thousands—even hundreds of thousands—of couples are practicing it and falling more in love with one another in the process gives us ample witness that it is practicable. NFP is providential.

Yes, it is providential. When Jesus made a promise, "I shall be with you all days even to the end of the world," He was promising to provide His Church with all she might need in every age to preach the Gospel effectively. I believe that through His Spirit, Jesus has poured into the world a consciousness of Natural Family Planning in this very crossroads of history where couples without NFP shall so often find it practically impossible to live in the state of grace.

Natural Family Planning is good news for marriages: it is necessary, it is helpful, it is practicable and it is beautifully providential.

Father David Grundman

I remember studying in the seminary the pros and cons and difficulties of Natural Family Planning. It's one thing to

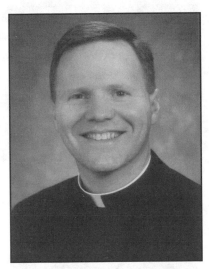

Father David Grundman
Pastor of three parishes, Diocese of
St. Cloud, Minnesota

truly know the method, but it is difficult to preach it. I had a lot of fears coming out of the seminary; but I was surprised, once I first started preaching the Word, at the receptivity of so many people out there. So many were truly open to it, and I received so many more thank-you's than comments from people upset with the message.

As I realized my limitations, I realized I also do have my part to play as a priest. I do my part as I preach the Word. In a sense, I get the ball rolling and hope couples start thinking more about this truth. They have various avenues to seek to learn more about NFP—brochures, Natural Family Planning offices, or other sources. I get it started as a preacher, and people look into it, and I believe that is what God is asking of me.

Bishop Fabian Bruskewitz

I am happy to be able to speak about NFP. I would point out, not only its positive values, but also how very important I have found preaching and teaching about NFP to be for the Catholics in the Diocese of Lincoln.

I have always found that it is exceptionally valuable to encourage people to understand the very positive aspects of the teaching of Pope Paul VI in *Humanae Vitae.* I try to illustrate how this papal teaching is a reflection of the constant doctrine of the Church. This teaching embodies not only God's revelation; it also embodies good solid conformity to the laws that God has set down in nature.

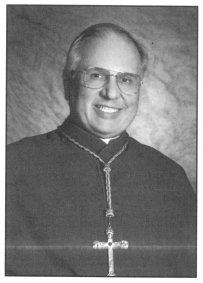

Bishop Fabian Bruskewitz
Diocese of Lincoln, Nebraska

Couples sometimes find it necessary to limit the size of their family. When they do so according to God's law, they find in their own marriage much more respect for each other, much more fulfillment, much less tension from even secondary concerns—money, addictions, and other kinds of problems that might affect the family function. This trend is not just anecdotal, but is statistically established. This experience underlines the great value of conforming to God's law in regard to family limitation.

The measure of happiness that a person wants to bring to a marriage is exceptionally important. In these days particularly, people are more inclined toward the natural, to being in conformity with nature. It is certainly not in conformity with nature, for instance, when the woman ingests very powerful steroid drugs that have unknown present and future repercussions on her health.

Of course, I also point out to priests especially, and to couples as well, that many artificial birth prevention methods are actually abortifacient. They have an anti-life aspect even beyond just closing the doors to the portals of creating new human life; they can actually involve the destruction of human life. Certain kinds of contraceptive drugs and IUDs are actually abortifacient elements, not simply contraceptive elements.

Monsignor Daniel Taufen

Thank you for taking the time to listen to these important messages. I applaud the bishops, priests, deacons, and Cardinal George who have so bravely proclaimed this important teaching of the Catholic Church. To order additional copies, please contact BOMA-USA at 651-699-8139 or via e-mail at boma-usa@msn.com.

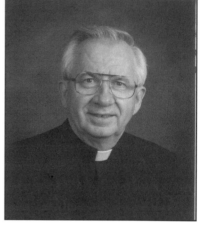

May God bless you with the wisdom and fortitude to speak the truth in this day when the message of *Humanae Vitae* and Natural Family Planning are so counter-cultural.

Monsignor Daniel Taufen, STL
Past Vicar General and Administrator,
Diocese of St. Cloud, Minnesota

June 2002

My Dear Brother Priests and Deacons:

This book is a compilation of transcribed taped messages from bishops, priests, and deacons throughout the United States, Mexico, Canada, and the Vatican.

It also includes a series of homilies that are most effective.

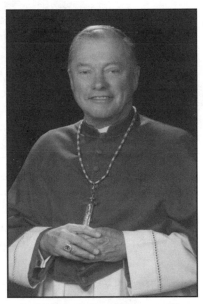

These two components have one thing in common: a message of love for our Church and a commitment to promoting Church teaching on Natural Family Planning.

The message is not always an easy one for some to share with the people in our faith communities, but it is important that we do so. If we can become more comfortable

Bishop John F. Kinney, Diocese of St. Cloud, Minnesota.

with this message, then we truly foster the concept of Natural Family Planning in accord with *Humanae Vitae*.

I hope that the sample homilies contained within this publication will be just the tools that will inspire you to begin talking with the people you serve.

Please use this book as you deem best for your particular community. I know you will find it well worth your time.

With kind personal regards, I remain,

Sincerely yours in Christ,

✠John F. Kinney
Bishop of Saint Cloud

OF HUMAN LIFE - A PASTORAL LETTER

A pastoral letter to the people of God of northern Colorado on the truth and meaning of married love.

✠ Charles J. Chaput, O.F.M. Cap.
Archbishop of Denver
July 22, 1998

Dear brothers and sisters in the Lord,

1. Thirty years ago this week, Pope Paul VI issued his encyclical letter *Humanae Vitae* (*Of Human Life*), which reaffirmed the Church's constant teaching on the regulation of births. It is certainly the most misunderstood papal intervention of this century. It was the spark which led to three decades of doubt and dissent among many Catholics, especially in the developed countries. With the passage of time, however, it has also proven prophetic. It teaches the truth. My purpose in this pastoral letter, therefore, is simple. I believe the message of *Humanae Vitae* is not a burden but a joy. I believe this encyclical offers a key to deeper, richer marriages. And so what I seek from the family of our local Church is not just a respectful nod toward a document which critics dismiss as irrelevant, but an active and sustained effort to study *Humanae Vitae*; to teach it faithfully in our parishes; and to encourage our married couples to live it.

I. THE WORLD SINCE 1968

2. Sooner or later, every pastor counsels someone struggling with an addiction. Usually the problem is alcohol or drugs. And

35

usually the scenario is the same. The addict will acknowledge the problem but claim to be powerless against it. Or, alternately, the addict will deny having any problem at all, even if the addiction is destroying his or her health and wrecking job and family. No matter how much sense the pastor makes, no matter how true and persuasive his arguments, and no matter how life-threatening the situation, the addict simply cannot understand —or cannot act on—the counsel. The addiction, like a thick pane of glass, divides the addict from anything or anyone that might help.

3. One way to understand the history of *Humanae Vitae* is to examine the past three decades through this metaphor of addiction. I believe people in the developed world find this encyclical so hard to accept not because of any defect in Paul VI's reasoning, but because of the addictions and contradictions they have inflicted upon themselves, exactly as the Holy Father warned.

4. In presenting his encyclical, Paul VI cautioned against four main problems (*HV* 17) that would arise if Church teaching on the regulation of births was ignored. First, he warned that the widespread use of contraception would lead to "conjugal infidelity and the general lowering of morality." Exactly this has happened. Few would deny that the rates of abortion, divorce, family breakdown, wife and child abuse, venereal disease and out-of-wedlock births have all massively increased since the mid-1960s. Obviously, the birth control pill has not been the only factor in this unraveling. But it has played a major role. In fact, the cultural revolution since 1968, driven at least in part by transformed attitudes toward sex, would not have been possible or sustainable without easy access to reliable contraception. In this, Paul VI was right.

5. Second, he also warned that man would lose respect for woman and "no longer [care] for her physical and psychological equilibrium," to the point that he would consider her "as a mere instrument of selfish enjoyment, and no longer as his respected and beloved companion." In other words, according to the pope, contraception might be marketed as liberating for women, but the real "beneficiaries" of birth control pills and devices would be men. Three decades later, exactly as Paul VI suggested, contraception has released males—to a historically unprecedented degree—from responsibility for their sexual aggression. In the process, one of the stranger ironies of the contraception debate of the past generation has been this: Many feminists have attacked the Catholic Church for her alleged disregard of women, but the Church in *Humanae Vitae* identified and rejected sexual exploitation of women years before that message entered the cultural mainstream. Again, Paul VI was right.

6. Third, the Holy Father also warned that widespread use of contraception would place a "dangerous weapon . . . in the hands of those public authorities who take no heed of moral exigencies." As we have since discovered, eugenics didn't disappear with Nazi racial theories in 1945. Population control policies are now an accepted part of nearly every foreign aid discussion. The massive export of contraceptives, abortion, and sterilization by the developed world to developing countries—frequently as a prerequisite for aid dollars and often in direct contradiction to local moral traditions—is a thinly disguised form of population warfare and cultural re-engineering. Again, Paul VI was right.

7. Fourth, Pope Paul warned that contraception would mislead human beings into thinking they had unlimited domin-

ion over their own bodies, relentlessly turning the human person into the object of his or her own intrusive power. Herein lies another irony: In fleeing into the false freedom provided by contraception and abortion, an exaggerated feminism has actively colluded in women's dehumanization. A man and a woman participate uniquely in the glory of God by their ability to co-create new life with Him. At the heart of contraception, however, is the assumption that fertility is an infection which must be attacked and controlled, exactly as antibiotics attack bacteria. In this attitude, one can also see the organic link between contraception and abortion. If fertility can be misrepresented as an infection to be attacked, so too can new life. In either case, a defining element of woman's identity—her potential for bearing new life—is recast as a weakness requiring vigilant distrust and "treatment." Woman becomes the object of the tools she relies on to ensure her own liberation and defense, while man takes no share of the burden. Once again, Paul VI was right.

8. From the Holy Father's final point, much more has flowed: In vitro fertilization, cloning, genetic manipulation, and embryo experimentation are all descendants of contraceptive technology. In fact, we have drastically and naively underestimated the effects of technology not only on external society, but on our own interior human identity. As author Neil Postman has observed, technological change is not additive but ecological. A significant new technology does not "add" something to a society; it changes everything—just as a drop of red dye does not remain discrete in a glass of water, but colors and changes every single molecule of the liquid. Contraceptive technology, precisely because of its impact on sexual intimacy, has subverted our understanding of the purpose of sexuality, fertility and marriage

itself. It has detached them from the natural, organic identity of the human person and disrupted the ecology of human relationships. It has scrambled our vocabulary of love, just as pride scrambled the vocabulary of Babel.

9. Now we deal daily with the consequences. I am writing these thoughts during a July week when, within days of each other, news media have informed us that nearly fourteen percent of Coloradans are or have been involved in drug or alcohol dependency; a governor's commission has praised marriage while simultaneously recommending steps that would subvert it in Colorado by extending parallel rights and responsibilities to persons in "committed relationships," including same-sex relationships; and a young East Coast couple has been sentenced for brutally slaying their newborn baby. According to news reports, one or both of the young unmarried parents "bashed in [the baby's] skull while he was still alive, and then left his battered body in a dumpster to die." These are the headlines of a culture in serious distress. U.S. society is wracked with sexual identity and behavior dysfunctions, family collapse and a general coarsening of attitudes toward the sanctity of human life. It's obvious to everyone but an addict: We have a problem. It's killing us as a people. So what are we going to do about it? What I want to suggest is that if Paul VI was right about so many of the consequences deriving from contraception, it is because he was right about contraception itself. In seeking to become whole again as persons and as a people of faith, we need to begin by revisiting *Humanae Vitae* with open hearts. Jesus said the truth would make us free. *Humanae Vitae* is filled with truth. It is therefore a key to our freedom.

II. WHAT *HUMANAE VITAE* REALLY SAYS

10. Perhaps one of the flaws in communicating the message of *Humanae Vitae* over the last thirty years has been the language used in teaching it. The duties and responsibilities of married life are numerous. They're also serious. They need to be considered carefully, and prayerfully, in advance. But few couples understand their love in terms of academic theology. Rather, they fall in love. That's the vocabulary they use. It's that simple and revealing. They surrender to each other. They give themselves to each other. They fall into each other in order to fully possess, and be possessed by, each other. And rightly so. In married love, God intends that spouses should find joy and delight, hope and abundant life, in and through each other—all ordered in a way which draws husband and wife, their children, and all who know them, deeper into God's embrace.

11. As a result, in presenting the nature of Christian marriage to a new generation, we need to articulate its fulfilling satisfactions at least as well as its duties. The Catholic attitude toward sexuality is anything but puritanical, repressive or anti-carnal. God created the world and fashioned the human person in His own image. Therefore, the body is good. In fact, it's often been a source of great humor for me to listen incognito as people simultaneously complain about the alleged "bottled-up sexuality" of Catholic moral doctrine, and the size of many good Catholic families. (From where, one might ask, do they think the babies come?) Catholic marriage—exactly like Jesus Himself—is not about scarcity but abundance. It's not about sterility, but rather the fruitfulness which flows from unitive, procreative love. Catholic married love always implies the possibility of new life; and because it does, it drives out loneli-

40

ness and affirms the future. And because it affirms the future, it becomes a furnace of hope in a world prone to despair. In effect, Catholic marriage is attractive because it is true. It's designed for the creatures we are: persons meant for communion. Spouses complete each other. When God joins a woman and man together in marriage, they create with Him a new wholeness; a "belonging" which is so real, so concrete, that a new life, a child, is its natural expression and seal. This is what the Church means when she teaches that Catholic married love is by its nature both unitive and procreative—not either/or.

12. But why can't a married couple simply choose the unitive aspect of marriage and temporarily block or even permanently prevent its procreative nature? The answer is as simple and radical as the Gospel itself. When spouses give themselves honestly and entirely to each other, as the nature of married love implies and even demands, that must include their whole selves—and the most intimate, powerful part of each person is his or her fertility. Contraception not only denies this fertility and attacks procreation; in doing so, it necessarily damages unity as well. It is the equivalent of spouses saying: "I'll give you all I am—except my fertility; I'll accept all you are —except your fertility." This withholding of self inevitably works to isolate and divide the spouses and unravels the holy friendship between them . . . maybe not immediately and overtly, but deeply, and in the long run often fatally for the marriage.

13. This is why the Church is not against "artificial" contraception. She is against all contraception. The notion of "artificial" has nothing to do with the issue. In fact, it tends to confuse discussion by implying that the debate is about a mechanical intrusion into the body's organic system. It is not. The Church has no problem with science appropriately intervening

to heal or enhance bodily health. Rather, the Church teaches that all contraception is morally wrong; and not only wrong, but seriously wrong. The covenant which husband and wife enter at marriage requires that all intercourse remain open to the transmission of new life. This is what becoming "one flesh" implies: complete self-giving, without reservation or exception, just as Christ withheld nothing of Himself from His bride, the Church, by dying for her on the cross. Any intentional interference with the procreative nature of intercourse necessarily involves spouses' withholding themselves from each other and from God, who is their partner in sacramental love. In effect, they steal something infinitely precious—themselves—from each other and from their Creator.

14. And this is why Natural Family Planning (NFP) differs not merely in style but in moral substance from contraception as a means of regulating family size. NFP is not contraception. Rather, it is a method of fertility awareness and appreciation. It is an entirely different approach to regulating birth. NFP does nothing to attack fertility, withhold the gift of oneself from one's spouse, or block the procreative nature of intercourse. The marriage covenant requires that each act of intercourse be fully an act of self-giving, and, therefore, open to the possibility of new life. But when, for good reasons, a husband and wife limit their intercourse to the wife's natural periods of infertility during a month, they are simply observing a cycle which God Himself created in the woman. They are not subverting it. And so they are living within the law of God's love.

15. There are, of course, many wonderful benefits to the practice of NFP. The wife preserves herself from intrusive chemicals or devices and remains true to her natural cycle. The husband shares in the planning and responsibility for NFP.

Both learn a greater degree of self-mastery and a deeper respect for each other. It's true that NFP involves sacrifices and periodic abstinence from intercourse. It can, at times, be a difficult road. But so can any serious Christian life, whether ordained, consecrated, single or married. Moreover, the experience of tens of thousands of couples has shown that, when lived prayerfully and unselfishly, NFP deepens and enriches marriage and results in greater intimacy—and greater joy. In the Old Testament, God told our first parents to be fruitful and multiply (Genesis 1:28). He told us to choose life (Deuteronomy 30:19). He sent His son, Jesus, to bring us life abundantly (John 10:10) and to remind us that His yoke is light (Matthew 11:30). I suspect, therefore, that at the heart of Catholic ambivalence toward *Humanae Vitae* is not a crisis of sexuality, Church authority or moral relevance, but rather a question of faith: Do we really believe in God's goodness? The Church speaks for her Bridegroom, Jesus Christ, and believers naturally, eagerly listen. She shows married couples the path to enduring love and a culture of life. Thirty years of history record the consequences of choosing otherwise.

III. WHAT WE NEED TO DO

16. I want to express my gratitude to the many couples who already live the message of *Humanae Vitae* in their married lives. Their fidelity to the truth sanctifies their own families and our entire community of faith. I thank in a special way those couples who teach NFP and counsel others in responsible parenthood inspired by Church teaching. Their work too often goes unnoticed or underappreciated—but they are powerful

advocates for life in an age of confusion. I also want to offer my prayers and encouragement to those couples who bear the cross of infertility. In a society often bent on avoiding children, they carry the burden of yearning for children but having none. No prayers go unanswered, and all suffering given over to the Lord bears fruit in some form of new life. I encourage them to consider adoption, and I appeal to them to remember that a good end can never justify a wrong means. Whether to prevent a pregnancy or achieve one, all techniques which separate the unitive and procreative dimensions of marriage are always wrong. Procreative techniques which turn embryos into objects and mechanically substitute for the loving embrace of husband and wife violate human dignity and treat life as a product. No matter how positive their intentions, these techniques advance the dangerous tendency to reduce human life to material which can be manipulated.

17. It's never too late to turn our hearts back toward God. We are not powerless. We can make a difference by witnessing the truth about married love and fidelity to the culture around us. In December last year, in a pastoral letter entitled "Good News of Great Joy," I spoke of the important vocation every Catholic has as an evangelizer. We are all missionaries. America in the 1990s, with its culture of disordered sexuality, broken marriages and fragmented families, urgently needs the Gospel. As Pope John Paul II writes in his apostolic exhortation *On the Family (Familiaris Consortio)*, married couples and families have a critical role in witnessing Jesus Christ to each other and to the surrounding culture (49, 50).

18. In that light, I ask married couples of the archdiocese to read, discuss and pray over *Humanae Vitae, Familiaris Consortio* and other documents of the Church which outline

44

Catholic teaching on marriage and sexuality. Many married couples, unaware of the valuable wisdom found in these materials, have deprived themselves of a beautiful source of support for their mutual love. I especially encourage couples to examine their own consciences regarding contraception, and I ask them to remember that "conscience" is much more than a matter of personal preference. It requires us to search out and understand Church teaching, and to strive honestly to conform our hearts to it. I urge them to seek sacramental Reconciliation for the times they may have fallen into contraception. Disordered sexuality is the dominant addiction of American society in these closing years of the century. It directly or indirectly impacts us all. As a result, for many, this teaching may be a hard message to accept. But do not lose heart. Each of us is a sinner. Each of us is loved by God. No matter how often we fail, God will deliver us if we repent and ask for the grace to do His will.

19. I ask my brother priests to examine their own pastoral practices, to ensure that they faithfully and persuasively present the Church's teaching on these issues in all their parish work. Our people deserve the truth about human sexuality and the dignity of marriage. To accomplish this, I ask pastors to read and implement the *Vademecum for Confessors Concerning Some Aspects of the Morality of Conjugal Life*, and to study the Church's teaching on marriage and family planning. I urge them to appoint parish coordinators to facilitate the presentation of Catholic teaching on married love and family planning —especially NFP. Contraception is a grave matter. Married couples need the good counsel of the Church to make right decisions. Most married Catholics welcome the guidance of their priests, and priests should never feel intimidated by their personal commitment to celibacy or embarrassed by the teach-

ing of the Church. To be embarrassed by Church teaching is to be embarrassed by Christ's teaching. The pastoral experience and counsel of a priest are valuable on issues like contraception precisely because he brings new perspective to a couple and speaks for the whole Church. Moreover, the fidelity a priest shows to his own vocation strengthens married people to live their vocation more faithfully.

20. As archbishop, I commit myself and my offices to supporting my brother priests, deacons, and their lay collaborators in presenting the whole of the Church's teaching on married love and family planning. I owe both the clergy of our local Church and their staffs—especially the many dedicated parish catechists—much gratitude for the good work they have already accomplished in this area. It is my intention to ensure that courses on married love and family planning are available on a regular basis to more and more people of the archdiocese, and that our priests and deacons receive more extensive education in the theological and pastoral aspects of these issues. I direct, in a particular way, our Offices of Evangelization and Catechetics; Marriage and Family Life; Catholic Schools; Youth, Young Adult and Campus Ministries; and the Rite of Christian Initiation for Adults to develop concrete ways to better present Church teaching on married love to our people, and to require adequate instruction in NFP as part of all marriage preparation programs in the archdiocese.

21. Two final points. First, the issue of contraception is not peripheral, but central and serious in a Catholic's walk with God. If knowingly and freely engaged in, contraception is a grave sin, because it distorts the essence of marriage: the self-giving love which, by its very nature, is life-giving. It breaks apart what God created to be whole: the person-uniting mean-

ing of sex (love) and the life-giving meaning of sex (procreation). Quite apart from its cost to individual marriages, contraception has also inflicted massive damage on society at large: initially by driving a wedge between love and the procreation of children; and then between sex (i.e., recreational sex without permanent commitment) and love. Nonetheless— and this is my second point—teaching the truth should always be done with patience and compassion, as well as firmness. American society seems to swing peculiarly between puritanism and license. The two generations—my own and my teachers'—which once led the dissent from Paul VI's encyclical in this country, are generations still reacting against the American Catholic rigorism of the 1950s. That rigorism, much of it a product of culture and not doctrine, has long since been demolished. But the habit of skepticism remains. In reaching these people, our task is to turn their distrust to where it belongs: toward the lies the world tells about the meaning of human sexuality, and the pathologies those lies conceal.

22. In closing, we face an opportunity which comes only once in many decades. Thirty years ago this week, Paul VI told the truth about married love. In doing it, he triggered a struggle within the Church which continues to mark American Catholic life even today. Selective dissent from *Humanae Vitae* soon fueled broad dissent from Church authority and attacks on the credibility of the Church herself. The irony is that the people who dismissed Church teaching in the 1960s soon discovered that they had subverted their own ability to pass anything along to their children. The result is that the Church now must evangelize a world of their children's children—adolescents and young adults raised in moral confusion, often unaware of their own moral heritage, who hunger for meaning,

community, and love with real substance. For all its challenges, this is a tremendous new moment of possibility for the Church, and the good news is that the Church today, as in every age, has the answers to fill the God-shaped empty places in their hearts. My prayer is, therefore, simple: May the Lord grant us the wisdom to recognize the great treasure which resides in our teaching about married love and human sexuality, the faith, joy, and perseverance to live it in our own families—and the courage which Paul VI possessed to preach it anew.

☩ Charles J. Chaput, O.F.M. Cap.
Archbishop of Denver July 22, 1998

IV. ADDENDUM: SOME COMMON QUESTIONS

In the weeks following publication of his pastoral letter, Archbishop Chaput answered some common questions about family planning and related issues in his regular Denver Catholic Register *column.*

1. Isn't a couple's method of family planning a matter of personal conscience?

Yes it is. Catholics, like all people, are always obligated to follow their consciences—on birth control and every other matter. But that's not where the problem lies. The problem lies in the formation of one's conscience. A conscientious person seeks to do good and avoid evil. Seeing the difference between good and evil, though, can sometimes be difficult. As Pope John Paul II has said, the basic moral law is written in the human heart because we're created in the image and likeness of God. But we bear the wounds of original sin, which garbles the message and dims our ability to judge and act according to truth.

Truth is objective. In other words, it's real; independent of us; and exists whether we like it or not. Therefore, conscience can't invent right and wrong. Rather, conscience is called to discover the truth of right and wrong, and then to submit personal judgments to the truth once it is found. Church teaching on the regulation of births, like all her moral teachings, is a sure guide for forming our consciences according to the truth. For we have the certainty of faith, as Vatican II reminds us, that the teachings of the Church on matters of faith and morals are "not the mere word of men, but truly the word of God" (*Lumen Gentium* n. 12). Too often, we use "conscience" as a synonym for private preference; a kind of pious alibi for doing what we want or taking the easy road. We only end up hurting others and ourselves.

2. I still don't see the big difference between a couple using "artificial" birth control and a couple using "natural" family planning. Don't both couples have the same intention, and isn't this what determines morality?

It's hard to see the difference when the emphasis is placed on "artificial" versus "natural" methods. People rightly point out that many things we use are artificial but not immoral. So it's important to realize that the Church doesn't oppose artificial birth control because it's artificial.

Rather, what the Church opposes is any method of birth control which is contraceptive, whether artificial devices, pills, etc., are used or not. Contraception is the choice, by any means, to sterilize a given act of intercourse. In other words, a contracepting couple chooses to engage in intercourse and, knowing that it may result in a new life, they intentionally and willfully suppress their fertility. Herein lies a key distinction: Natural Family Planning (NFP) is in no way contraceptive. The choice to abstain from a fertile act of intercourse is completely different from the willful choice to sterilize a fertile act of intercourse. NFP simply accepts from God's hand the natural cycle of infertility that He has built into the nature of woman.

Regarding the issue of intention: Yes, both couples may have the same end in mind—to avoid pregnancy. But the means to achieve their common goal are not at all alike. Take, for example, two students, each of whom intends to excel in school. Obviously that's a very good intention. With the same goal in mind, one studies diligently. The other cheats on every test. The point is, the end doesn't justify the means—in getting an education, in regulating births, or in anything else.

3. I'm a priest. If I preach about what's wrong with contraception, I'll lose people.

Let me turn that around: If priests don't preach the Church's message about contraception, heaven loses people. Don't be afraid. When Jesus preached the truth, He lost people. But, little by little, He gained even more people. Take courage in the Lord.

It shouldn't surprise us that people find this teaching hard to accept. Every Gospel-based life has things which are hard to accept. Should we stop teaching the truth because it's difficult? Of course not. We have the joy and the responsibility before God to preach the truth lovingly in season and out of season. The Church won't be renewed without a renewal of family life. And the family can't be renewed without a return to the truths taught in *Humanae Vitae*. Ignoring this issue can't be an option: In the long run, its cost is too high. Therefore, we should make every effort to better understand the importance of Church teaching in this regard, and witness to it boldly and with confidence.

4. In your pastoral letter, you said that the most intimate, powerful part of each person is his or her fertility. My husband and I are unable to have children. What does this mean for us?

Many couples bear a great cross because, despite their openness to life, they're unable to have children. But marital love is always life-giving when spouses give themselves honestly to each other, even if a child isn't conceived. Only when husband and wife intentionally withhold their fertility, or abuse their sexuality in some other way, can we speak of a "life-less" act of intercourse.

Spouses' self-giving in one flesh remains the most intimate, powerful and life-giving expression of their love for one another, even when nature, or some problem of nature, prevents new life from being conceived. Medical technology can sometimes correct a physical problem, allowing a child to be conceived by the loving embrace of parents. This is a proper and wonderful use of technology. However, couples should remember that, as creatures themselves, they're not the arbiters of human life. Ultimately, no one is free to manipulate the conception of a human person. No matter how sincere a couple's intentions, many of today's new procreative techniques treat human life as a product which can be manufactured—and in doing so, they violate human dignity. Again, the end never justifies the means.

Children aren't the only way a marriage can be fruitful. If God, in His design, closes one option for a couple, He will open another. Their love can find expression in adoption, foster-parenting, or dozens of forms of apostolic work. This kind of counsel, of course, is much easier to give than to accept willingly. I would never want to understate the real pain and loss felt by infertile couples. But I know, both from faith and from my friendships with married couples over the years, that if a husband and wife choose to trust God, their love will always be rewarded with fertility and new life—if not in the form of a child, then in the way they impact the world around them.

5. Why is the Church so obsessed with sex?

You know the old saying about the pot calling the kettle black—well, here's a great example. Questions like this one may very well be honest, but they conceal where the real obsessions lie. American society is drowning in a sea of disordered sexuality. In such circumstances, it's hardly an "obsession" for the Church to speak clearly and forcefully about how to swim. It's her responsibility and mission.

God created our sexuality to be a sign in the world of His own life and love, and to reveal to us that we can only fulfill ourselves by loving as He loves. When sexuality becomes distorted, however, it's no longer able to communicate God's life and love. Empty of true love, life lacks meaning, and people soon seem disposable. Sex becomes a pursuit of selfish gratification at the expense of others. Children are no longer welcomed as the natural fruit of married love, but are seen as a burden to be avoided. We don't even shrink from killing (through abortion) thousands of innocent preborn lives a day in satisfying our convenience and appetites.

It's no exaggeration, then, to say that disordered sexuality is the beginning of what Pope John Paul II calls "the culture of death." In fact, we'll never build a culture of life and love without first restoring the true meaning of human sexuality. If the Church is so concerned about sex, it's because she seeks to defend the dignity of the human person, and to safeguard the true meaning of life and love which sexuality is meant to reveal.

6. How can I preach against contraception and praise the virtues of NFP? As a priest, I'm not married.

First, the truth is the truth, no matter who speaks it. Second, preaching isn't about the preacher; it's about the message. Third, in his promise of celibacy, a priest doesn't forget or deny his sexuality. Instead, he dedicates it to a different—but equally fertile—kind of fruitfulness. In other words, priestly celibacy is an affirmation, not a rejection; a strength, not a weakness. It's a "yes" to God which enables us to understand and serve our people better.

Remember that marriage, religious life, the single vocation, and the priesthood are all designed to fit together and complement each other in the life of the Church. Each needs the other. Each, in its own proper way, fulfills the fundamental human vocation to give ourselves away in love. I think we priests often underestimate how effective our pastoral counsel can be on issues like contraception. People want and need the truth, and over time, the human heart naturally responds to it. But our people can't respond if they don't hear the message of *Humanae Vitae* faithfully and persuasively from their pastors. That's our job, and we should embrace it joyfully.

HOMILIES

Francis Cardinal George

Dear Sisters and Brothers in Christ,

God is very unfair by our standards, because everything from God is gift. It's all gift, and gifts are not equally shared. The parable of the laborers in the vineyard makes it clear that there is something that doesn't agree with our standard of equal pay for equal work when the master of the vineyard calls people early in the morning to work and ends up giving them the same pay, exactly, as those who join at midday, or even at the end of the day and work very little indeed.

It seems that God is arbitrary. But He's not arbitrary; He's just extraordinarily generous. The other side of that story of God's generosity is in the parable that we just heard proclaimed today as a result of Peter's question to the Lord: "How many times should I forgive someone who harms me?" He was talking about real harm, not just a hurt feeling. There was a great discussion in the schools, among the rabbis, as to how often one is called, according to the law, to forgive; three, four times?

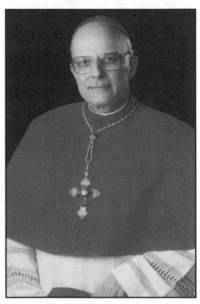

His Eminence Francis Cardinal George, OMI
Archdiocese of Chicago, Illinois

It's a good thing that Peter asked these questions

and that he had enough trust in the Lord to put himself on the spot in this way. Jesus responded to Peter's questions with this parable showing that God's love is infinite, God's love is generosity, God's love is pure gift. And along with that love comes pardon.

We are a bundle of gifts, all of us. Life itself is pure gift. We didn't ask to be born; we don't earn our life, our existence. But that life comes with some deadly strings attached. Human life is marked by sin and by sin's consequence, death. Along with the gift of life, therefore, comes the gift of a Savior who, out of God's pure generosity and love, comes to save the world from our sinfulness, both inherited and personal. In baptism comes the gift of new life in Christ. We are reborn on the basis of God's infinite forgiveness, on the basis of God's merciful pardon.

We say, and rightly so, that it was a marvelous miracle on the part of God to create something out of nothing. For the question of creation is far less how, and how long, and its process, and the rest, than the simple statement that there would be nothing to develop or evolve unless God had created something out of pure nothingness. Out of His own love, out of His own generosity, He wills the world into existence, and He maintains it in existence through His providence. Without God's sustaining power, everything would resolve back into nothingness. And yet, as marvelous is God's creating something out of nothing, how much greater, as St. Augustine says, is it to create good out of evil. Something out of nothing: a great miracle. Good out of evil: a far greater miracle.

That unlimited pardon that can take sin and create mercy, create love where there was hatred, is symbolized in this parable where the Lord presents a master who is owed millions of dollars by a very ordinary servant who could not make, perhaps, more than a couple of thousand a year. When the servant says, "Have patience and I'll repay you," it's really rather absurd. The master knows that and, having pity on the man and not wishing to destroy him and his family, he forgives the entire debt.

But that forgiveness on God's part, that mercy, is not sentimental toleration of hurtful behavior. We have to become part of God's generosity, we have to, in our turn, pardon others and give them new life from Christ in our own imitation of God's generosity. It isn't enough to just say, "Everything is forgiven," without calling sin what it is. What is also clear is that it is sinful to search for any kind of vengeance, to look even at wrongs that are truly against us with a sense of vindication. We have been humbled first by our own being forgiven and, out of that sense of our own powerlessness before our own sinfulness, of our own inability to break the habits of sin without the power of God's grace, comes a sense of righteousness—but never self-righteousness. Our righteousness comes only from the gift of God's grace, the gift of God's love.

Among all the gifts that God gives us, life and love always come together; they can never be separated. Nor can they can be separated in the gift of human sexuality. Life and love, generosity and pardon, always come together. Perhaps some of you are old enough to remember that movie and book, *Love Story.* It was popular when I was much younger, and it contained a famous last line: "Love means never having to say you're sorry." Rather, love means always saying you're sorry because, as you grow in love, you discover how you offend the one you love. You know how it is. When you're first married, you don't know which buttons to push to make someone angry or upset, but after a few years you know very well. And that's how it is in our love affair with God. As we grow closer to the Lord and experience his own infinite love—and with that, the pardon of our own sinfulness, which we are utterly incapable of escaping without his generosity and love—then the greatest of saints keep saying we are the greatest of sinners. And they are, in the sense that they know the demands of love, they know the nature of God and, therefore, they know the destruction and death that comes from sin.

When love and life, when generosity and pardon, are separated, especially in the gift of human sexuality, when they are separated biologically, then all kinds of perversions arise. Marriages which are arranged only to produce heirs—that is one perversion. Marriages that are gone through only to provide a legal formula for sterile cohabitation—that is another perversion. Love and life in God go together. Generosity and pardon are one. And we who are made in God's image and likeness must keep them together in our life and in our love, in everything we think and say and do.

Good comes out of evil in God's love. Even the situation that we're faced with today around contraception has enabled the Church to deepen her understanding of the gift of human sexuality. For many centuries, the evilness, the sinfulness of artificial contraception of any sort was based largely upon a consideration of the biological end, the *finis*, of the marital embrace. Because a natural end was thwarted, it was a sin against the natural law, and that still is true. But with Paul VI, in *Humanae Vitae*, that sense of natural law was expanded. He begins to speak about contraception as a sin against the values of human life. There is an expanded vision of sexuality now because of the challenge that the Church was meeting.

In the Pontificate of John Paul II and in his Magisterium, which is so touched by his personalist philosophy, there is a further deepening of the theological argument in the Church's development of her understanding of the gift of human sexuality. The pope explains that contraception is a sin against the nature of the marital embrace itself as total self-giving, a sin against generosity and, therefore, a sin against life itself.

In Paul's letter to the Romans that we've just heard, we understand that life is always other-directed. Directed first of all to our Master, Jesus Christ, whose disciples we claim to be. We always live and die, not for ourselves, but for Him. That's basically what God is telling us when he gives us the gift of human sexuality in the covenant of marriage: husband and wife live and die for one another.

There has been, in these last decades, a great coarsening not only of behavior but also of vocabulary, starting with the Kinsey Report in which sexuality wasn't regarded as other-directed, wasn't regarded as directed toward the transmission of life, wasn't regarded even as a means to increase love of another person. Kinsey spoke of a sexual outlet rather than a person. There is no otherness in that perspective. Talk and entertainment and behavior have been so terribly cheapened that, in fact, in a post-Freudian culture, it is very difficult to talk about chastity at all because it's immediately seen as a form of repression, and that is a far greater sin than promiscuity.

A woman talked to me recently about our not preaching about male chastity. We just talk about abortion, we talk a little bit about contraception, maybe—very little, far too little —but we don't talk about male chastity, and she made me think. When I was growing up, I was taught that you're supposed to honor women, that you're supposed to have respect for women. I don't know whether or not young boys, young men, are taught that any longer. Perhaps it's because people see it as a relic of an age of chivalry, which was a way perhaps, in their interpretation, of putting women down by keeping them in an honored place.

Whatever the reason, there is a loss of the sense that man is capable, with the help of God's grace, of even shaping his own biological urges according to the rhythms of his wife's body. That is honor, that is respect; and it transforms a marriage. Not without difficulty, as you know far better than I, not without pain and enormous problems at times but, in the end, as I saw myself in many of my pastoral conversations with very poor farm workers, a marriage is transformed.

People who talk about the Church as, in some sense, the enemy of women haven't thought things through. If the social and sexual teaching of the Catholic Church defined our behavior in this society, there would be no rape. There would be no abandoned wives or children. There would be no spousal abuse. There would be no abortion, no adultery, no fornication. Who would be the losers if the social and sexual doctrine of the Catholic Church, and of many other Christian bodies, were in fact, normative for our behavior? Lots of entertainers and a handful of pundits and politicians. Who would win? Women, and men who love them and love them well.

The GIFT Foundation is itself a great gift, and I want to thank you for creating this gift. It follows, I think, on an understanding of what Vatican II said about the relationship between Church and the way in which the Church is to be a leaven in society, to transform society, transform it by attending to God's universal call to holiness—not holiness as a kind of a ghetto reality, not holiness reserved to a class or a caste, but holiness which is universal. We won't all be equally holy, for it's a gift, God's grace, God's love; but that doesn't matter. We are loved according to the way God sees fit to love us, and that is more than enough. The call to love and to holiness is truly universal. That is the foundational teaching of the Second Vatican Council.

In that perspective, it is lay people who are to work to make the world holy, becoming holy themselves through the gifts of Christ that are available through his body, the Church. It is my obligation as bishop to see that the means to holiness are made available in the Church. But the teaching of the Church, once delivered to the laity, is to be worked out in their areas of specialization and competence.

That is what, it seems to me in reading your program this weekend, you have done: a marvelous working out on the part, largely, of lay men and lay women of their own areas of specialization—in such a way that the teaching, once expressed clearly, is able to be followed in terms and in ways that make sense to the laity around us. I cannot do that; you have to do it. It's a gift, and I'm very grateful to you for it.

I ask forgiveness in the light of the gospel of today for the fearfulness of pastors who very often will not speak to this issue. Sometimes because they don't totally accept the teaching of the Church; but more often than not because they are worried about the unity of the flock. Priests try very hard to keep people together. And you have to understand that and be sure that your own conversations with them are not touched with any kind of self-righteousness which would destroy the world of gifts in which we live. The bishop and the priests are primarily concerned about unity and, therefore, in that very conservative role of trying to keep people together, sometimes we don't advance as quickly as we should.

What we sometimes forget is that the unity is not around priests and bishops. The unity is around Christ, whose mouthpiece we are to be and, therefore, whose truth, including the full truth about the gift of human sexuality, must be preached, but in ways that will not totally destroy the unity of the flock we have to keep together around Christ. Our pastoral judgment is a prudential judgment, and we can be wrong in deciding not to speak. But understand it for what it is, and pray that priests will have the courage necessary to preach and teach, in season and out, about the nature of life and love, the gift of human sexuality. For that gift and for your gifts and for all gifts, we thank God today as we celebrate the gift of the Eucharist. God bless you.

Used with permission of the Gift Foundation.

Natural Family Planning
and the New Evangelization
Bishop Raymond Burke

Embracing Natural Family Planning goes contrary to our culture. It insists upon respect for the integrity of the marital act, according to God's plan, in a society which believes that one may manipulate the marriage act, as if God did not exist, in order to eliminate its essentially life-giving nature. NFP couples are concerned for the integrity of man and woman who stand always before God. Grounded in an integral vision of the person who is called both to a natural and earthly life, but also to a supernatural and eternal life, Paul VI affirmed that the teaching of the Church "is founded upon the inseparable

Bishop Raymond Burke
Diocese of LaCrosse, Wisconsin.

connection, willed by God and unable to be broken by man on his own initiative, between the two meanings of the conjugal act: the unitive meaning and the procreative meaning."

Married love is a gift from God to man and woman, who are stewards of the gift, called to bring it unstained into the fullness of life in Heaven. Pope Paul VI instructs us so simply and profoundly in the matter when he teaches: "Marriage is not, then, the effect of chance or the product of evolution of unconscious natural forces; it is the wise institution of the Creator to realize in mankind His design of love. By means of the reciprocal personal gift of self, proper and exclusive to them, husband and wife tend towards the communion of their beings in view of mutual personal perfection, to collaborate with God in the generation and education of new lives."

It is critical that the theological foundation of Natural Family Planning, found in the Church's teaching about man and woman, be more and more understood. Too often, NFP couples have the sense of being alone in living according to this truth. Too often, too, even those who are supportive speak as if you are in possession of some highly specialized knowledge when in fact, these truths are open to all.

So much remains to be done to evangelize the whole Church about NFP and its place in the proclamation of the whole Gospel of Life. I am constantly amazed at the number of Catholics who fail to recognize that contraception is at the first entry into the culture of death and, more practically, that many of the contraceptive chemicals and devices are, in fact, abortifacient.

Here it must be stated that Catholic institutions, especially Catholic healthcare institutions, can be of great assistance to the Church in her work of assisting couples to grow stronger in conjugal chastity and to be responsible parents. Catholic institutions, worthy of the name, always seek ways to be more fully part of the Church's mission. With regard to Natural Family Planning, Catholic clinics and hospitals will assist the Church by making certain that the medical care provided to spouses is coherent with Church teaching and by providing the forum for the teaching of Natural Family Planning and for providing qualified assistance to couples who encounter special difficulties in conceiving a child. Because of the thorough-going secularization of our society, it is key that no countersigns to the Church's teaching be given by Catholic institutions.

In his apostolic letter "Novo millennio ineunte," at the end of the Great Jubilee of the Year 2000, Pope John Paul invited us to "put out into the deep" for a catch, as he invited the Apostle Peter to do at Lake Gennesaret. Peter and his companions had been fishing all night without any result, but, at the command of our Lord, they put out the nets once again for a catch which was so great that their nets nearly broke. Our Lord also commands us to "put out into the deep," to put aside our fears and discouragement and to trust in Him. "Putting out into the deep" means taking up the apostolate entrusted to us with new enthusiasm and energy in the confidence that our Lord, in His time, will bring forth the good fruits of our labors.

In fact, in light of the many challenges presented by our culture to teaching the Gospel, our Holy Father urges us to engage in a new evangelization - teaching and living the Gospel as if for the first time, as if it had never before been preached in our land. He urges us to have the enthusiasm and energy of the first disciples who were ready to accept a martyr's death in order to remain faithful to Christ and the Gospel. He urges us to consider the lives of the saints throughout the Christian centuries and in our own time, and to remember that the call to holiness of life is given to all. As he states, the ideal of perfection must not be misunderstood as if it involved some kind of extraordinary existence, possible only for a few "uncommon heroes" of holiness. The ways of holiness are many, according to the vocation of each individual. "I thank the Lord that in these years he has enabled me to beatify and canonize a large number of Christians, and among them many lay people who attained holiness in the most ordinary circumstances of life."

I believe that now is the time to repropose the high standard of Natural Family Planning to everyone as the way to holiness of life in marriage and the family. Holding up the high standard of ordinary Christian living in the matter of conjugal chastity—always open to the exchange of love and the potential to co-create new life with God—will lead spouses to discover anew the great dignity of their vocation to the married life and the sanctity of the marriage act as an expression of the vocation.

The virtue of married chastity which entails the full respect for the life-giving and love-giving nature of the conjugal union is the Christian way of life for all couples, not just for a few who are striving for heroic sanctity. In this regard, the Church must take care that the preparation of couples for marriage and the pastoral care of those who are married include full instructions regarding Natural Family Planning. On the day of their marriage in Christ, a couple receives the vocation and the grace to respond to the vocation of faithful, lasting, and life-giving love with each other. The "big" Church, in her care for the "little" Church, must prepare couples to embrace their vocation as fully as possible and to respond faithfully to their vocation throughout the years of marriage, which God gives them.

To carry out the apostolate of Natural Family Planning in our culture which often is indifferent and even hostile to the Gospel, requires unity and competence on the part of those who instruct others in Natural Family Planning.

Again in *Novo millennio ineunte*, our Holy Father counsels us against any naive expectation that the new evangelization can be carried out by finding some magic formula or new program. Instead, the formula and program is Christ and the Gospel, revealing the fullness of God's truth and love to us. Following Christ in this way begins with prayer, our daily conversation with Him, which has its origin and its highest expression in the Sunday Eucharist. Closely united to the Holy Eucharist is regular access to the Sacrament of Penance with which we seek the conversion of our life and the grace to begin anew in the way of the cross which leads to life. Frankly, there is no way that we can carry out the new evangelization except in Christ, with whom we have communion through prayer and public worship. This emphasis on prayer reminds us that it is God's grace which inspires and makes possible the new evangelization. It is fatal to our mission to forget that "without Christ we can do nothing."

The second way of the new evangelization is "to nourish ourselves with the word in order to be 'servants of the Word' in the work of evangelization." Reading the word of God, the study of the Scriptures as they are understood by the Church, will keep us on track with Christ in a globalized society, in which there is an easy blending of cultures and religions that might compromise the truth of Christ and the Gospel.

In the teaching of Natural Family Planning, the Catholic Church gives prophetic witness. It points to the radical demands of life in Christ for those called to the married life. The other Christian denominations have abandoned this perennial teaching on contraception, according to what had been the understanding of the Word of God and the Christian Tradition, up to a few decades ago. We must continue to nurture our apostolate at the font of the Holy Scriptures and the Church's Tradition in order to be faithful to Christ and to give prophetic witness, with Him, to the truth about married love.

I close with words of our Holy Father in *Novo millennio ineunte* which confirm us in our service of the Gospel of Life: "At a time in history like the present, special attention must also be given to the pastoral care of the family, particularly when this fundamental institution is experiencing a radical and widespread crisis. In the Christian view of marriage, the relationship between a man and a woman—a natural and total bond, unique and indestructible—is part of God's original plan, obscured throughout history by our 'hardness of heart,' but which Christ came to return to its pristine splendor, disclosing what had been God's will 'from the beginning.' Raised to the dignity of a sacrament, marriage expresses the 'great mystery' of Christ's nuptial love for His Church." Through faithful living in accord with the wisdom embodied in Natural Family Planning, may more and more couples give faithful and generous expression to the truth of their married love, "the 'great mystery' of Christ's nuptial love for his Church."

Humanae Vitae Thirty-third Anniversary Commemoration
Fourteenth Sunday C—July 7, 2001
Bishop Joseph F. Naumann

I
Thirty-third Anniversary of *Humanae Vitae*

I am pleased to welcome to the Cathedral tonight those associated with the Archdiocesan Department for Natural Family Planning as well as members of the Natural Family Planning Association. Each year the Natural Family Planning Network in the Archdiocese sponsors a liturgy in July to commemorate the anniversary of the promulgation by Pope Paul VI of his Encyclical Letter, *Humanae Vitae*—On Human Life. This July 25 marks the thirty-third anniversary of the promulgation of *Humanae Vitae*.

Bishop Joseph F. Naumann, auxilary bishop, Diocese of St. Louis, Missouri

On behalf of Archbishop Rigali, I express gratitude to all of you who are involved with the promotion of the complete teaching of the Church on married love and life. I thank you for the powerful witness of your lives as married couples to the truth of the teaching contained in *Humanae Vitae*.

71

The promulgation of *Humanae Vitae* thirty-three years ago occasioned sharp criticism from within and without the Church. It was said then, and it is repeated today, that *Humanae Vitae* demonstrated the lack of understanding by those with teaching authority in the Church of the realities of human love and human sexuality. Pope John Paul II has on numerous occasions reaffirmed the doctrine contained in *Humanae Vitae*. Critics of *Humanae Vitae* offer, as evidence of its errors, polling data revealing a large portion of Catholics disagreeing with the Church's teaching regarding artificial contraception.

It is in this context of commemorating the anniversary of this important and yet controversial teaching that we reflect on today's scripture readings for the Fourteenth Sunday in Ordinary time.

II
God Desires Joy for His People

One of the central themes of today's readings is the joy the Lord desires for his people. In our first reading from Isaiah, the Lord expresses his desire to comfort his people like a mother comforts her child. The prophet, in describing the joy of God's people, uses the imagery of a child in the safe comfort of a mother's arms who is delighted with being nourished at her breasts.

Recently, I was at a gathering where a mother with a young infant asked me to hold her baby so that she could take a picture of me with her baby. I was happy to comply with her request, but I cannot say the same for her baby. No matter how

I struggled to create a comfortable position for the baby, he wailed and was inconsolable. I am sure that he could sense my lack of experience and competency in holding him and this added to his distress, but I think largely my crime was that I was not his mother.

It was amazing to see his transformation as soon as I returned him to the familiar and comforting arms of his mother. It was instant joy.

I have always been amused when visiting in homes of friends how children love to be on their mother's lap. This is not just true of infants and toddlers and small children. I have seen more than once, teenagers almost crush their poor mothers as they plop themselves on their laps—half in jest but half in an unarticulated desire to return to those simpler and securer days when they spent a good deal of time in their mothers' arms.

III
Our Joy Is Not in Our Productivity, but in Our Identity as Beloved Sons and Daughters of God

In today's gospel, we see Jesus commissioning the seventy-two to go forth and prepare the way for his coming by proclaiming the Gospel message. The passage concludes by describing their return and the disciples' expressions of joy and enthusiasm at the healing God effected through them. Jesus counsels them not to make their joy dependent on any perceived power they possess or the apparent positive effects of their ministry. Jesus tells them their joy is that their names are written in heaven, in other words that they are beloved sons and daughters of the Father who has prepared an eternal home for them.

The message for us is clear—the Lord's desire is the greatest and most profound joy for his disciples. It is a joy that is not dependent on our accomplishments or achievements. It is a joy that is not bestowed upon us by the acceptance or the approval of those with power and authority in this world.

It is a joy that comes from the goodness of God. It is a joy that is based on our identity in Him, not our productivity in the world. Our joy is derived from being made in His image, from being so loved by Him that Jesus came into the world to fully share in our humanity. God so values us that the Son of God gave His life for us. Through the grace of our baptism our names are indeed written in heaven where the Lord has prepared our eternal home.

It is a joy that no matter what the turmoil of the exterior circumstances of our life, we are resting in the loving and comforting arms of our God. Whether the world may criticize or mock or reject or ignore us makes no difference, we are as content as a child in the arms of his mother. We have the joy of a child on her mother's lap, who knows and only cares that she is the delight of her mother.

IV
Adversities Allow Us to Connect with the Cross of Jesus

Thus, Jesus could dispatch the disciples for their mission without many resources, as lambs among wolves, knowing that some and perhaps even many would not welcome them or their message. It was their task to bring Jesus' message of peace and hope and healing to as many who would receive it with open hearts. They were not to argue with those who chose not to listen or retaliate against those who were hostile to the Gospel message.

They were not to take a poll to see what most people wanted to hear them say and change the Gospel message to conform with popular opinion. They were simply to move on and try to reach others whose hearts were disposed to the truth and life contained in their preaching and teaching.

In fact, like St. Paul, even our adversities become a source of joy for us for they allow us in some small way to connect with the cross of our Lord Jesus. They are reminders to us of the depth of his love for us. They provide us with opportunities to give witness to our appreciation for what Jesus endured for us as we strive to transform our human suffering with the same love and faith that he evidenced on Calvary.

V
Eucharist Reaffirms Our Identity

These readings for us today invite us to discover anew the sheer joy of understanding ourselves to be brothers and sisters with Jesus and through him beloved daughters and sons of the Father. Each time we come to Mass, this central truth of our faith is reaffirmed. We encounter again the love first revealed on Calvary, the love of Jesus Christ willing to give his life so that we might have life.

We receive anew the living presence of Jesus in communion and are renewed in our Christian identity as living temples of God and members of the Body of Christ. This is the source of our strength and our joy, and no one and nothing in this world can deprive us of it.

VI
Challenge to Be Open to God's Plan for Marriage

Our liturgy also offers a challenge to each of us. For those of us today who have not been open to, have not understood, or even rejected the Church's teaching on the dignity of human life and the joy and responsibility of human love, we are being called to open our hearts to these important truths taught by our Church under the guidance of the Holy Spirit.

We do not want to be like those who closed their hearts to the teaching of Jesus and his disciples. We do not want to be counted among those people and places where the disciples were instructed to shake the dust from their feet.

So many who have rejected this teaching have never really heard it, or never had the time—or made the time, to understand its rationale. In *Humanae Vitae*, Pope Paul VI acknowledged some of the reasons many would have difficulty accepting this teaching. He respects the good intentions and legitimate concerns for the emotional and physical well-being of married couples who at times are overwhelmed with the responsibilities of parenthood. The Pope acknowledged authentic concerns about problems of poverty in nations where population is the densest. Yet, in the end he reminded us of the simple truth that we cannot seek to do a good with an evil means.

VII
Thirty-Three Years of Experience
Affirms the Teaching of *Humanae Vitae*

When you compare what those who advocated thirty-three years ago for the moral permissibility of artificial contraception predicted would happen in our society to what Paul VI in *Humanae Vitae* prophesied, it is readily apparent who understood the implications of what was being chosen. When you look at what has actually transpired during the past thirty-three years, it is hard to deny the vision of Paul VI and the wisdom of his teaching.

Advocates for artificial contraception asserted that access to contraception would strengthen marriages by relieving the pressure of additional children and the limitations on couples' opportunities to express their love through sexual intimacy. They were convinced sexual experience before marriage would help make the choice of a marriage partner better and, therefore, marriages stronger. They predicted a dramatic decrease in unwanted and problem pregnancies. We were told that abortion would disappear because with no more unwanted pregnancies the need for abortion had been eliminated.

Paul VI, on the other hand, expressed concerns that the widespread use of artificial contraception would result in lower moral standards. He predicted an increase of pornography, sexual activity before marriage, and adultery. He saw the reliance on artificial contraception bringing about a general weakening of marriage and family life. In *Humanae Vitae*, Paul VI even predicted what has actually occurred in China governmental policies imposing contraception and abortion. Paul VI foresaw a diminished respect for the human person and an increase in reliance upon abortion as the back-up to failed contraception.

With 1.3 million abortions annually in our nation, a persistent high level of teen pregnancies, a higher and higher number of single-parent families, pornography that is cabled into our living room, a divorce rate that more than doubled and remains at fifty percent today, it is difficult not to admit the accuracy of Paul VI's concerns. Similarly, one can only conclude that advocates for contraception were either clueless or deceptive in their prognostications about the consequences of artificial contraception.

VIII
Couples Evangelizing the World for Christian Marriage

The last thirty-three years have brought about a great refinement in Natural Family Planning methods providing a morally acceptable means for couples to make responsible decisions, while being respectful of the balance God created in linking human fertility and sexual intimacy. The statistical effectiveness of Natural Family Planning, when a couple believes it is best for their marriage and family to make choices to avoid a pregnancy, is impressive. The less than five percent divorce rate for couples using Natural Family Planning speaks volumes about how Natural Family Planning improves couple communication, intimacy, and mutual respect. The many previously infertile couples that have been able to conceive a child assisted by the knowledge of the fertility cycle and hormonal treatments are an important part of the good news of Natural Family Planning.

The strongest and most effective affirmation of the truth of *Humanae Vitae* is not statistics and numbers but the couples present at Mass this evening and many like them throughout the archdiocese who are living daily the teaching of *Humanae Vitae* with fidelity and joy. Your marriages and your families are living testimonies that marital and family happiness will be found by honoring God's plan for married love and life.

You are very much like the disciples in the Gospel today who were sent two by two to proclaim the good news. Your married love and joy are a beautiful proclamation of the good news about God's plan for marriage and family life.

In *Humanae Vitae*, Paul VI challenged married couples to do exactly what you are doing—to live their marriage covenant with love and joy thus evangelizing other couples to the wisdom of God's plan for marriage. Paul VI recognized artificial contraception as the beginning of a troubling process of human beings attempting to seize control of the life-giving process. Today, with in vitro fertilization, researchers calling for the ability to experiment with tissues of discarded embryos, advocates for human cloning becoming more shrill in their demands, the use of genetic screening to produce designer children, we are reaping the consequence of what was unleashed with the acceptance of human intervention to destroy the balance that God had created in uniting sexual intimacy and the life-giving process.

Conclusion

Our liturgy today challenges each one of us to reconsider or reaffirm our commitment to the truths contained in the prophetic teaching of *Humanae Vitae*. Each of us in accord with our state of life and particular responsibilities must strive to do whatever we can to communicate the good news about Christian love and marriage. In an age that is so attuned to what is natural and suspicious about the human manipulation of nature, we must communicate anew the folly of employing chemical warfare on a woman's fertility and the tragedy of surgical interventions to render men or women infertile.

Each one of us needs to become witnesses for chaste love, using the great gift of our human sexuality in a way that is proper and appropriate for our state of life. We need to communicate in word and action that only chastity provides the true plan to healthiness and happiness in our human relationships.

The world may consider us foolish and mock us. We need not be afraid for even in the midst of struggle and adversity, we know that in following the Lord's way we are placing ourselves in the arms of God. Perched on his lap what else do we need? Nothing can deprive us of His peace and His joy.

"Responsible" Parents Are Open to Life
by Most Rev. J. Peter Sartain,
Bishop of Little Rock, Arkansas

This is the fourth article in a wonderful series on the transmission of life and responsible parenthood as printed in The Arkansas Catholic. *Reprinted with permission. (Bishop Sartain is from Memphis, TN and served as Vicar General of the Diocese of Memphis and Pastor of St. Louis Church before his appointment as Bishop of Little Rock.)*

In an often-quoted and often-misunderstood section of the letter to the Ephesians, St. Paul begins a passage about wives and husbands with these words: "Be subordinate to one another out of reverence for Christ." (Ephesians 5:21).

In the late fourth century, St. John Chrysostom suggested that young husbands should say to their wives: "I have taken you in my arms, and I love you, and I prefer you to my life itself. For the present life is nothing, and my most ardent dream is to spend it with you in such a way that we may be assured of not being separated in the life reserved for us . . . I place your love about all things, and nothing would be more bitter or painful to me than to be of a different mind than you" (Homily on Ephesians 20:8).

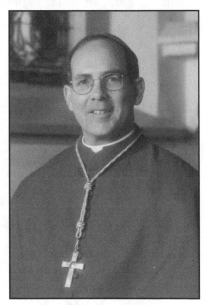

Bishop Peter Sartain
Diocese of Little Rock, Arkansas

John captured well Paul's teaching that wives and husbands are to be subordinate to one another—in other words, they are to consider the other's good as of greatest importance, they are to sacrifice for one another as Christ himself has done, and as a couple they are to see themselves as subject to Christ. The concept of mutual subordination is a way of expressing the particular kind of love which characterizes Christian marriage, which is a "union of loves" so complete that two become one.

In the Roman Catholic Church, it is ordinarily understood that husband and wife are ministers of God's grace and confer on one another the sacrament of matrimony by declaring their consent before the Church. They are chosen instruments of God in one another's lives—and not just the day of the wedding, but "until death do us part." They are literally to help one another get to heaven! Moreover, their vocation entails not only being one in love for each other, but also being God's instruments as a couple, most especially instruments of his creative power in giving life to children. Their love looks beyond itself and seeks to raise up new lives.

These two meanings or values of Christian marriage—the "unitive" and "procreative"—are intimately, inseparably, linked; they cannot be divided without affecting the couple's spiritual life and compromising their marriage and the future of their family. In fact, if a person enters marriage with the deliberate intention to exclude children from the marriage, the consent is invalid. Just as the persons of the Trinity are "fruitful" in love for one another and in creation, so the love of husband and wife is intended to be fruitful in love and offspring. Married couples are cooperators in the love of God the Creator and are, in a certain sense, its interpreters.

Being "cooperators" and "interpreters" of the creative love of God carries both extraordinary joys and extraordinary responsibilities. An especially intimate and personal responsibility of every couple is making decisions about the regulation of births. Just as the crown of creation was human life, so the supreme gift of marriage is a human person, and the vocation of husband and wife entails honoring this capacity of their love with special care.

The Church does not teach that couples should have a certain number of children, but it does offer teaching about responsible parenthood, which can be summarized in these five points:

1. Husbands and wives have a responsibility to understand and honor the "wisdom of the body," including its biological processes. I have discovered in marriage preparation sessions through the years that many young people (especially men) are not well informed about the biological aspects of human reproduction.

2. Humans share certain instincts and passions, and Christians are to guard and control them through reason and will.

3. Taking into consideration the physical, economic, psychological and social conditions of their marriage, couples exercise responsible parenthood by a prudent and generous decision to raise a large family, or by a decision (for serious reasons and made according to the moral law) to avoid a new birth for the time being, or even for an indefinite period.

4. Responsible parenthood has its roots in the truth about "right and wrong" established by God, and spouses have a duty to inform their consciences and make decisions according to this truth. Husbands and wives recognize their duties toward God, themselves, their family and society, and are called to maintain a proper set of priorities.

5. Offering their marriage in discipleship to the Lord Jesus, couples do not make purely arbitrary or subjective decisions regarding becoming parents but use the wisdom of God as their guide. As in every other aspect of their lives, Christian couples always remain open to God's wisdom and providence regarding family life, including the size of their particular family. Since God brought them together and shares his love with them, he will always guide them along the paths that are best for them.

Interwoven among these aspects of responsible parenthood is the understanding that the two great meanings or values of marriage—the "unitive" and "procreative"—are never separated. A love that is complete and faithful, a love which holds nothing back from the other, will remain open to God's creative plan. After all, it is God's love in the first place.

"Human Life," Thirty-Three Years Old
Bishop Thomas J. Olmsted

From *Catholic Advance*, the Official Newspaper of the
Diocese of Wichita, Kansas, Friday, July 20, 2001.
Reprinted with permission.
(This piece was originally written for the thirty-third anniver-
say of *Humanae Vitae*, which was on July 25, 2001.)

On July 25 this year, "Human Life" reaches the age of
thirty-three; that is, the encyclical of Paul VI better known by its
Latin title, *Humanae Vitae*. Now,
after more than three decades,
the fruits of this prophetic
encyclical are beginning to come
into view. It's not unlike what
happened 2000 years ago. After
thirty-three years of earthly life
and a public ministry that met
increasing hostility, Jesus laid
down his life on the cross and
then rose in unexpected glory.
That first Easter morning,
Christ brought new life to the
world. Even though very few

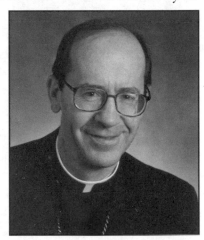

Bishop Thomas Olmsted, D.D.
Diocese of Wichita, Kansas

perceived the new beginning, human history had been transformed; the long reign of sin had ended: redemption was at hand.

The fruits of *Human Life*, after thirty-three years, are
budding forth in a variety of places: teens are rediscovering the
good news of chastity; couples are turning to Natural Family
Planning, while more physicians are trained to assist them;
engaged couples are finding that Catholic teaching on marriage is

a source of joy, not a burden. Best of all, formerly contracepting couples are coming to a new appreciation of motherhood and fatherhood, rooted in the gifts of fertility and conjugal love.

It should not surprise us that, just when Jesus rose from the dead, many people did not initially see the wisdom of *Human Life*, for the teaching of *Human Life* is as deep a mystery as Christ Himself. Christ teaches us that what seems a cross in fact reveals a new dimension of life. Christ's self-offering on the cross remains God's gift to the human family, a gift that teaches us how sacrifice can bear great fruit.

The encyclical *Human Life* had been issued at ground zero of the sexual revolution, which was then sweeping across North America and Western Europe. Its message was decidedly counter culture. It predicted, with amazing accuracy, the dire consequences of a widespread contraceptive mentality: increased marital infidelity, sex considered a recreational commodity, corrosion of respect for human dignity, especially of women, and the use of abortion and contraception as tools for states to control population growth without respect for the rights of couples. The catastrophic consequences of irresponsible sex are evident all around us. We see more clearly today not only that contraception is wrong, but that because contraception is wrong, it has bad consequences.

More importantly, the positive consequences of *Human Life* are now in evidence. For it set in motion a fresh way of thinking about conjugal love. It lifted our vision to God's perspective, to His plan to bring children into the world through a love that is total, faithful, exclusive, fruitful and truly human.

Building on the broad strokes of *Human Life*, John Paul II, in the early 1980s, elaborated a more comprehensive theology of sexuality and marriage. He explained how the human body—male and female—has a nuptial meaning; that is, how the body is capable of making visible what is invisible, how the body is a kind of sacrament of God's Trinitarian life. Thus, conjugal love participates in God's life and love and shares it with the world. John Paul also showed how the nuptial meaning of the body gives a sense of purpose and mission to a couple, whereas contraception falsifies the marital embrace.

The '80s and '90s also saw great advances in research on holistic methods of birth regulation which are verifiably more effective than contraception and fully respectful of the natural meaning of conjugal love. The knowledge we have today about a built-in set of fertility signals placed in the female body by our Creator liberates couples from old-fashioned methods. New holistic methods offer couples much greater knowledge of their fertility and give them medically proven natural means of cooperating with God in the procreation of human life. In addition, as John Paul II points out, family planning by observing nature's biological rhythms is "the only method of fertility regulation that respects the dignity and equality of the spouses as persons."

We stand now on the brink of a new fruitfulness. The sexual revolution that has birth control technology at its core is collapsing around us. A positive and ennobling understanding of sexuality and of marriage is emerging on the foundation of *Human Life*.

Thank God for the courage of Paul VI. Thank God for his prophetic wisdom. As *Human Life* reaches thirty-three years of age, the harsh winter of the contraceptive mentality is ending; springing forth afresh is an appreciation of sexuality as a gift from God that enriches married couples, ennobles family life, and reflects the very image of the Triune God.

Monsignor James D. Conley
Official in the Congregation for Bishops,
Vatican City State

(Homily given on October 17-18, 1992, for the beginning of Natural Family Planning Week, on the Respect for Life theme of "Natural Family Planning: The Choice for a Healthy Marriage.")

Today we observe the beginning of Natural Family Planning week throughout the Diocese of Wichita. It is "natural," so to speak, that we highlight Natural Family Planning during the month of October, a month the United States Catholic bishops have designated as, "Respect Life Month." The theme for this year is: "Natural Family Planning: The Choice for a Healthy Marriage."

Monsignor James Conley
Official in the Congregation for Bishops
Vatican City State, Italy.

The Scriptures teach us the value of perseverance. Moses persevered in prayer and remained steadfast against great odds and, thereby, was delivered from his enemies. In a gospel parable, Jesus speaks of the widow who kept persisting in her cause for justice and pleading with a corrupt and unbelieving judge. In the end, the judge gave in to her pleas and ruled in her favor. Jesus teaches us the "necessity of praying always and not losing heart."

Not losing heart in living up to our Church's clear and consistent teaching on marriage and human sexuality requires perseverance and steadfast prayer. This is particularly true today when we live in a culture that is dominated by a "contraceptive mentality." Jesus' words to us about the "necessity of praying always and not losing heart" must be taken seriously by all people but especially by married couples who today are trying to be faithful to the message of the gospel, against "great odds."

It is a sad reality that the use of artificial contraception is widely practiced today. What is even more tragic is that some Catholic couples use contraception as a method of family planning, and some Catholic physicians do not hesitate to recommend the use of birth control and even prescribe contraception to their patients. The Catholic Church has consistently taught and continues to teach that the use of artificial contraception in all its forms, including direct sterilization, is "gravely immoral" and is contrary to the law of nature and nature's God.

Artifical contraception is always considered immoral; however, there is a morally acceptable way by which married couples may space the births of their children and even postpone a pregnancy for an indefinite period of time. For "good and sufficiently serious reasons," spouses may regulate births by abstaining from the marital act during the wife's easily identified fertile periods. This exercise of "responsible parenthood" is known as Natural Family Planning. Recent scientific research has so refined the methods of Natural Family Planning that, today, couples may practice responsible parenthood in ways that are altogether reliable (ninety-nine percent effective), medically safe without harmful side effects, and morally acceptable.

When couples give their mutual consent to be spouses in the holy sacrament of Matrimony, they give themselves to each other and to God in a holy bond of love. This mutual self-donation is expressed most completely in the marital act itself, which is a renewal of the marriage covenant. The God-given meaning of the marriage act is realized in the union of the spouses and the openness to new life. The Church teaches that these "unitive" and "procreative" meanings of conjugal love must never be separated and must always be respected.

When Natural Family Planning is used to avoid a pregnancy or to space the number of children when there are justifying reasons to do so, it is free of the detrimental moral and physical elements which are so intrinsic to artificial methods. Natural Family Planning is a method of spacing births that fully respects the beauty of human sexuality according to the design of God. But NFP is more than a technique of family planning: it is actually a way of life. It is a method which is shared fully by both husband and wife. It respects the personhood of the spouses and the dignity of the marital act. No doubt, Natural Family Planning involves a measure of sacrifice and at times self-restraint, but it can also lead to greater self-mastery and mutual respect. Additionally, it gives rise to a creativity in developing new ways of communicating love and showing affection.

Just as Jesus Christ put no conditions or reservations on His love for us, so married couples give themselves totally and unreservedly to each other in the bond of marriage. This totality of giving, which is required of conjugal love, is rooted in a deep faith in God's providential love and care for his people.

In the second reading from St. Paul to Timothy, St. Paul encourages his listeners to remain faithful to the full message of the Church, a message we must preach in season and out, whether convenient or inconvenient. Natural Family Planning is not the easier route consistently paraded by the contraceptive mentality of our society. But it is the most love-generating and life-giving way to live the mystery of married love. Strength for doing so is found in "praying always and not losing heart."

Prayers of the Faithful for Natural Family Planning Sunday

1. In gratitude to God for the gift of our sexuality. May all persons use this gift wisely according to their state in life and in accordance with your holy will. (Response)

2. For all married Catholics, that they may have the courage to accept and be faithful to the Church's consistent teaching on marriage and Natural Family Planning. (Response)

3. That God will bless all those married couples who are wanting to achieve a pregnancy. (Response)

4. That God will comfort all those parents who have lost a child through miscarriage or stillbirth. (Response)

5. That all husbands and wives will be faithful to their marriage covenant and deepen their love for one another. (Response)

6. For young people and all single people, that they will have the moral courage to resist the temptations of today's culture, and live chaste lives in Christ. (Response)

7. That Church leaders and Catholic physicians will actively promote Natural Family Planning to the people they serve. (Response)

Monsignor Bob Guste:
Our Lady of Perpetual Help, Kenner, Louisiana

There was a time years ago when one might sometimes hear the complaint: "All they ever talk about from the pulpit is sex!" Today the chances are you would hear the opposite: "When are we going to hear a sermon on sexual morality?" Well, be disappointed no longer. Here we go—specifically on the subject of contraception.

Monsignor Bob Guste
Ministry of Evangelization and Spiritual Renewal

The first thing I want to say is that the Catholic Church is not against family planning! Does that surprise or shock you? It is true. She is for responsible family planning. The Church affirms that every child is a precious gift of God— more valuable than the entire material universe—to be welcomed as Jesus welcomed them. "Let the children come to me," He said, "and do not prevent them; for the kingdom of heaven belongs to such as these" (Mark 19:14). The Church recognizes, however, that there are at times serious reasons for married couples to avoid or postpone another pregnancy. Because of this, the Catholic Church around the world is the largest promoter of Natural Family Planning. Modern-day Natural Family Planning has been perfected way beyond the old calendar Rhythm Method and is as effective as all the ongoing contraceptives and more effective than some. It does not require a regular menstrual cycle and is based on any one of a number of easily observable bodily signs that indicate the comparatively short period each month when a woman is fertile. Once learned, it costs no money to use and has none of the side effects that are associated with almost all of the other methods—especially the chemical ones. A September 1993 article from the *British Medical Journal* reports on studies of NFP's effectiveness in various parts of the world. It cites one study from India where almost 20,000 women used the Billings Ovulation Method of Natural Family Planning. There were almost no pregnancies among these women. The doctor who authors the article proposes that Natural Family Planning is the way for the world to go.

A 1995 study, however, of U.S. Catholic women between the ages of fifteen and forty-four shows about sixty-eight percent using some form of contraception or sterilization. The chances are that many of them think that what they're doing is all right.

Twenty years ago, listening to and sympathizing with the struggles that many married couples faced, I was inclined to go along with their thinking. In any case, I would have told them, out of compassion, that it was up to them to make a conscientious decision, after considering everything.

Of course, every moral decision is meant to be made in the sanctuary of our consciences—but what is conscience? If not stifled by emotion, it moves us to seek the truth and follow it. *Now*, with all my heart, I urge couples to form their consciences in the light of reason and faith, of Christ and His Church. I tell them what the Catholic Church clearly teaches, has always taught, and what the official Catechism of the Church repeats: God is the creator of man and woman, marriage and sex, and contraception is a serious misuse of His creation. I say this with no less compassion than before. True compassion and love, however, call us to proclaim the truth, the full good news of God's plan for our lives.

Many things have brought me to the point where I no longer hedge on this issue. One is a new appreciation of the urgent need for attention to the Church's teaching mission in a world that has lost a sense of any objective right or wrong or even of objective truth itself. Related to this are the disastrous consequences of the "make up your own mind" or the "form your own conscience" directive. It's been used to justify everything under the sun.

Did you know that before 1930 all the Christian denominations were in agreement about the evil and sin of contraception? Protestant denominations after the Reformation still stood shoulder to shoulder with the Catholic Church on the subject for about 400 years. It was only in 1930 that one denomination, the Anglican bishops at their Lambeth Conference in England, reluctantly made some exceptions in condemning contraception. This was the beginning of the collapse of other Christian denominations on this issue, and then on other aspects of sexual morality and abortion as well. A crack had been made in the dike of clear sexual moral teaching, and the whole wall began to crumble.

When the Pill first came out in the sixties, many, like myself, thought we had struck upon a great new invention. How wrong we were! The endless list of possible side effects, spelled out on the physicians' package insert with the Pills, should alarm anyone. A former president of Pharmacists for

Life says he hasn't met one otherwise healthy woman on the Pill who has not experienced some ill effect from it. At least thirty pecent of women on the Pill discontinue its use after the first year. Later came Norplant, the five-year under-the-skin contraceptive implant. Countless women have complained and even made legal claims of harm from the device. In Louisiana alone, as of October 2001, thousands of women are attempting a class-action suit in court against the Norplant producers.

It was this kind of information that prompted me to rethink the whole birth-control issue. Specifically, it began to happen at a medical-ethics workshop with a presentation by a brilliant Latin American woman on the effectiveness and benefits of modern-day Natural Family Planning contrasted with the harmful effects, physical, psychological and spiritual, of unnatural birth control. The most alarming part of this presentation, however, was the fact that not only the IUDs but *all* the chemical contraceptives (including *all* the Pills, Norplant, and contraceptive Depo-Provera injections) have a possible abortive effect.

They normally stop ovulation but not always. They all allow for some breakthrough ovulation. Because of this, couples can sometimes conceive, that is, the egg can be occasionally fertilized. All of the DNA is present; human life begins. All of these chemicals, however, alter the lining of the uterus so that it is not prepared as it normally would be to receive this newly conceived human being. The chances are that these one-week-old, tiny new lives would be sloughed off and destroyed. Medical literature and the physicians' package insert for Pills will confirm this and other possible harmful effects, but most people never read them. That is what prompted over 200 doctors toward the end of the twentieth century to sign what is called "A Declaration of Life" affirming the abortive potential of all the above-mentioned chemical contraceptives. There was also a report on contraception submitted at the 1990 International Congress of the World Federation of Doctors Who Respect Human Life that included something about spermicides. It cited information presented at a graduate medical seminar about the chemical Nonoxynol-9 contained in spermicides (creams, sprays, sponges, etc.). By a different mechanism, it can also have an abortive effect. Condoms are often coated with spermicide.

For me, all this was like nature's red light warning: "Something's wrong with contraception; something's right with Natural Family Planning." It also showed me how, long before the Pill, the Church's ancient teaching was prophetically safeguarding not only marriage and sex but respect for women and human life itself. The Church isn't behind the times; she's way ahead of the times!

What is the main reason, however, why contraception is wrong? It is wrong because it is human interference in an area that is God's domain. "From the beginning," Jesus said, "the creator 'made them male and female.'" (Matthew 19:4) God made marriage. He made sex, and it needs to be respected and exercised in the way He intended. In sharing with us the power to give life, He joined it to an intimate expression of self-giving love. To interject a barrier or chemical to separate the act of love from its possible life-giving effect is to tamper with and seriously violate a sacred design of God.

Let me give an example. Suppose you sit down to eat a delicious meal, but before doing so, you put an obstruction in your throat to catch the food. You still get the taste of eating and the socializing that may go with it, but then you take the obstruction after you're finished and throw it in the garbage can. Sorry if it seems crude, but what's the difference between that and using condoms, Pills or doing anything that—one way or the other—blocks, destroys, or interferes with the natural life-giving effect of the marriage act? When Natural Family Planning is used, however, the couple is not abusing but *using* nature. They do not interfere with a sacred God-designed process, but, by self-control, make use of the natural rhythm of fertile and non-fertile days as designed by the Creator. By choice they either use or don't use their marital rights on those days. To continue the eating analogy, periodically, you can either eat or fast, but when you choose to eat, you can't deliberately frustrate its life-giving effect. The same is true of sex.

Another way of looking at it, less graphic and more subtle, is this: Sexual intercourse is meant to express the total gift of oneself to another without anything being held back. As the Second Vatican Council put it, the marriage act should "by objective standards . . . preserve the full sense of mutual self-giving and human procreation in the context of true love." It is intended by God to be an expression and renewal of the couple's marriage agreement and covenant. It is God's way for them to say to each other over and over again, "I take you and give myself to you for better, for worse, for richer, for poorer, in sickness and in health, without reservation, until death." In the use of contraceptives of any kind, a couple is not saying this unreservedly. There is a hidden agenda, a holding back, a conditional consent: "I am giving myself to you but not completely." It is like putting a hood over your head before embracing and kissing your spouse!

The marital union, modeled on the union of Christ and His Church, is a call to total unselfish self-giving and holiness.

St. Paul exhorts the Christians of Ephesus (Ephesians 5:25-26), "Husbands love your wives, even as Christ loved the Church and handed himself over for her to sanctify her . . ." Unnaturally blocking fertility (an integral part of who a person is) in the marriage act itself always contradicts the complete self-donation and holiness (wholeness) of the act.

All this would also (and even more so) apply to permanent sterilization for the purpose of birth control, carrying with it the added evil of unjustified bodily mutilation. The more than one million sterilizations a year in the U.S. are not without their own harmful side effects, physical, psychological, and spiritual.

To sum up, God created the marriage act for two main purposes: to bear children and to express and deepen the union of husband and wife—and He put these two purposes together. Contraception contradicts both purposes and pulls them apart. The reason that it is so wrong and in itself a serious evil is because it violates what otherwise in itself is so good and sacred. The Catholic Church is not down on sex. It is just the opposite. The Catholic Church is preserving and proclaiming the beauty, the rightness and true meaning of what God has created.

There is much more that could be said on this issue, but other sources are available. Among them, I strongly recommend Dr. Janet Smith's talk on cassette "Contraception: Why Not?" as one of the best presentations on the subject.

The most discussed document on the subject is Pope Paul VI's encyclical, *Humanae Vitae*, (*Of Human Life*), issued in 1968. It affirms a teaching that goes back in the Church to early ages, about the sacredness of the marriage act and the immorality of interference with it.

When I was first exposed to this encyclical, I was so influenced by the news commentators and the protesting theologians that I didn't think that much of it. Years later, when the smoke had cleared and I read it calmly, thoughtfully, and with an open mind and heart, I was deeply impressed with the profound wisdom and love in it. It is like the young guy who said, "You know, when I was eighteen, I thought my dad was pretty stupid. But when I got to be twenty-one I was amazed how much he had learned in three years!"

I realize now that if I have trouble accepting some solemn teaching of the Church, I should not presume that she just has not gotten "with it" or that I have some special insight that this Church of 2000 years has not yet considered. Instead, why not presume that I am the one who has not yet caught up with the teaching Church or plumbed the depth of her wisdom and insights? Make the effort to pray, to study, and to consult those who are with the Church on the issue. The witness of Natural Family Planning couples is powerful—especially of converts from contraception. With an overall divorce rate estimated at fifty percent in the United States, committed NFP couples rarely divorce. They often talk about relationships, including the sexual relationship, that are greatly improved, and about family life greatly blessed with a new peace and happiness. This is God's amazing grace at work in those who open their lives, especially their most intimate life, to Him.

Jesus Christ sent out His Church with the commission to "make disciples of all nations . . . teaching them . . ." and the promise, "I will be with you always . . ." (Matthew 28:19-20). He called the Church ". . . the light of the world . . . a city set on a mountain . . ."(Matthew 5:14.) Without that light of Christ and His Church, we could argue endlessly about what is right and what is wrong—what God wants us to believe and to do on the way to eternal salvation—and still walk in doubt and darkness. But as the bishops of the world proclaimed at the Second Vatican Council, "The Church is, by the will of Christ, the teacher of the truth. It is her duty to give utterance and authoritatively to teach that Truth which is Christ Himself and also to declare and confirm by her authority those principles of the moral order, which have their origin in human nature itself.

What the Church teaches is not politically correct and goes against the current of public opinion, and many of us, the priests, have failed to clearly preach it. Thank God, however, that the Catholic Church officially down through the ages has remained faithful to the truth in opposing contraception.

Especially through the voice of the successors of St. Peter, she continues to call the world back to God's plan for man and woman, for life, for sex, and for marriage. Pray that we can all hear that call, live it, rejoice in it and share it with everyone.

Reverend Ronald Lawler, O.F.M., Cap.

One of the constant objections to Natural Family Planning is that it asks too much of people. Many will acknowledge its positive features as a form of family planning: it reverences life, is never abortifacient; it has no deadly side effects; it demands only a moderate amount of abstinence. Still!—it requires self-denial and self-discipline of a kind that ordinary people will not put up with. At the bottom line, this logic says, it won't work.

But this objection fails to appreciate what an "ordinary person" can and will do—given a motive and loving help. The New Testament portrays Christ as actually demanding far greater things of people than Natural Family Planning does. Everywhere he appears pastoral and

Father Ronald Lawler, O.F.M., Cap. Director of Religious Education—Adults and Families, Diocese of Pittsburgh, Pennsylvania, author of **Teaching of Christ** and other works.

compassionate, understanding about human weakness. For that very reason, everywhere he made great demands. "Is divorce permissible for any cause?" This was asked by legal minds expecting a legal answer in accord with somewhat lenient Jewish divorce practice, but the question evoked a stunning answer. "What God has joined together, let no man put asunder."

The objection comes back: "But Moses said . . ." That was no answer to him. "From the beginning it was not so." It was the hardness of hearts that had generated laxity in this matter of principle. And our human hearts do tend to be hard. Still Christ did not despair of us and find technological ways to solve problems while our hearts remain unaltered. He demanded and made possible newness of heart. His own disciples were stunned at this sexual ethic. "If what you say is true," they marvel, "it is not good to marry at all!"

Implicit in the apostles' protest was the lament, "You don't understand." Throughout the gospels there seems a readiness to acknowledge that the Christian teaching on sex and love seems incredible to the unconverted heart. To live as husband and wife until death is a grand ideal. Mere common sense can dismiss difficult ideals. But in its suffering when the ideals are not pursued, the modern world may be ready to hear again and to understand Christ, who makes seemingly difficult demands in order to be kind and lead us to greatness.

Moral theology ought always be written with remembrance of the sublime vocation of the "ordinary person." Its task is not to make life easy in the flabby and self-destructive sense but to help make a good life possible. In the light of the gospel, ordinary people are called to greatness and made capable of it by grace, as the very meaning of their lives. Marriage is a sign of the love between Christ crucified and his Church. It is both a grand and frightening vocation. It cannot be lived unless people make efforts toward love that is like Christ's; that is, unless they let him make them begin to be great.

Natural Family Planning takes the dignity of ordinary men and women seriously. It is sensitive to their needs and has experience of their weakness. But it knows how splendid is the greatness that can spring up in the human spirit. In fact, it is for the sake of this goodness and greatness that the universe was made.

In the gospels, openness to the truth is central to goodness and greatness of heart. Our times are days of image-making and advertising, days of rhetoric, propaganda, days of untruth. There is always a temptation when faithfulness to known truth would be demanding, to be false to the truth and the truly good one knows. This is not out of any direct contempt for truth, but there can be a kind of willingness to be not quite open to the truth. Such an attitude would be opposed to the truthful joy of Catholic faith. Beyond the obscurities of human confusion, Christ dwells always in the family of faith, and by his Spirit guides us into all the truth. He teaches us what love requires and gives strength to do it.

When there is too great a concern to find "pastorally tolerable," that is, soft and undemanding ways of living Christianity, a terrible price is paid. Then priests begin to hear the terrible words we now hear too often: "We don't know what our faith teaches anymore." We are inclined to be silent, fainthearted, even unsearching, caring little about what the truth that we are to live in love might be.

This truth is revealed to us in the inner sanctuary of conscience, where we are alone with God whose voice echoes in the depths of our hearts. For Catholic faith, conscience is not a mere subjective norm, an inner voice that a man has a right to follow in contradiction to what he is able to realize is God's law. Rather, the truly conscientious person must always be truly seeking what is really God's will, whatever it may cost. Such a person desires earnestly never to confuse personal preferences with the call of God. If we find that, no matter what we contemplate doing, the Lord always agrees with us, we can be sure we have a bad connection. For our conscience to be a reliable moral guide, it must be formed by God's wisdom revealed through His Scriptures as interpreted by His Church.

It is true that people must be free to make their own decisions, for only in freedom can we truly act as persons made in the divine image. But freedom and responsibility to choose truthfully are not opposed. We have a duty to choose what really is good, to the extent that God enables us to know the good. The Church maintains great openness to diverse views whenever that is suitable. Many moral questions are infinitely complex. When revelation and the earnest reflection in faith has led us to no decisive teaching, the Church always calls for freedom. But when the Church has taken a decisive position, then scholars, and indeed all the faithful, have a duty to give religious assent. Those who believe that Christ really dwells in the Church as a teacher, and that His spirit guides it into the truth, are ready to say yes when the Church insistently proposes a moral teaching which expresses the convictions of the long-standing lived experience of a Church guided by the Spirit of Christ. Even if some theologians dissent, they are easily refuted by the most brilliant moral thinkers of our time who teach in communion with the Magisterium.

Often such dissent arises from genuine pastoral concern about the difficulties of couples and families. But that genuine concern does not confer validity on any argument made in its name. It is possible to be kindly and sincerely wrong. The moral revolution in the Church was not based on any real grounding in serious scripture scholarship, in investigations and tradition or in rational developments in moral theory. It was based on a mistaken sense of pastoral compassion and on the forlorn hope that someone will provide justification for what people are now urged to do. This is a frail footing for those who would stand against what the fathers and doctors and saints have always said, and against what experience and faith have taught us as necessary for honoring the dignity of man and of human love.

The task we have to do for the Church is so over-whelmingly important that we cannot be content with small successes and self-righteousness. For all our frailty, God has given us something needed in the whole family of faith and the whole human family. Let us acknowledge our responsibility.

We must ask God to make us and our leaders long for greatness and goodness of heart. Our vocation to become Christians is a serious one. With such a vocation, you are called to help the world, and to do this you must lean on Christ and draw from him the courage to carry out your vocation faithful-ly. God has not given us heroic models like John Paul II and Mother Teresa simply so that we might admire them. You too must be flames of fire. For the whole world wants and yet resists what God calls you to give it. So you must give gener-ously, from the greatness of heart that Christ will create in you, and with you.

Sacred Scripture
Father Daniel McCaffrey, STD

"Proclaim the message, insist on it, in season and out of season, refute falsehood, correct error, call to obedience, but do all with patience and sound doctrine. (2 Timothy 4:2)

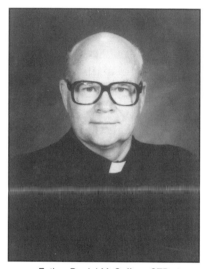

Father Daniel McCaffrey, STD
Director, Natural Family Planning Outreach
Oklahoma City, Oklahoma

Father Bede Jarrett, a twentieth-century English Dominican warned priests that they would lose their people for two reasons:

1. By not praying for them.

2. In failing to correct their faults.

In light of this, today, I'm going to speak on a few very sensitive subjects, seldom if ever, spoken about from the pulpit. They are the sins of contraception and sterilization.

Your first reaction may be one of surprise or even anger due to the recent clerical scandals. You might even cry out, "put your own house in order before condemning our sins." This reaction is very understandable and demands an honest answer.

Father Richard John Neuhaus answers that if bishops and priests had proclaimed the teachings of the Catholic Church and had lived according to their sacred vows, there would be no scandal. Please pray for your pastors!

In spite of this, St. Paul says, we pastors have the duty to proclaim the Apostolic teaching, especially when it comes to married life. It is in and through this sacred state that Almighty God normally bestows on humanity His blessings and graces. As you know well, marriage was instituted by God Himself. Jesus Christ added to its dignity by elevating it to a sacrament. The union of husband and wife is sacred indeed. John Paul II likens married life to the divine embrace of God the Father and God the Son and also to the Holy Spirit who proceeds from this love.

St. Paul, in his letter to the Ephesians, instructs husbands to love their wives as Christ loves his Church. Our Lord's love for his Church is all consuming unto the pouring out of the last drop of his blood. We are the fruits of that love. His love for His Church is true and total—not contraceptive; and married love, which is based on this, must be no different. The act of love between husband and wife is sacred and should be treated as such. It represents something far beyond itself.

Christianity has always taught that the unitive and procreative aspect of this union must never be separated. Love and openness to life are two aspects of the one act. Contraception breaks up this integrity and offends seriously against the sixth commandment, which pertains to chastity, without which one is not pleasing to God.

Sterilization, e.g. vasectomy and tubal ligations, destroys those sacred powers given to a man and women which allows them to cooperate with God in bringing new life into the world. It is a serious violation of the fifth commandment to respect life.

The Church realizes the obligation to regulate family size, if there is a serious reason to do so, but it always recognizes children to be the crown of the marriage and that large families are a special blessing. At the same time, God has given to the Church a new medical breakthrough called Natural Family Planning. It's not the old rhythm method and it is ninety-eight to ninety-nine percent effective. It respects the way God created a woman, it promotes intimacy, encourages communication, and among people who use NFP, the divorce rate is extremely low, some say less than five percent as compared to the fifty percent found among the general population. (Let the people know of the availability of NFP in the Diocese/Parish at this point)

This is not a marginal issue.

1. Spiritual life—the sins of contraception and sterilization stunt Christian growth. Naturally so, because the commandments are being broken. Statistics indicate that the vast majority of Catholics disagree with the Church's teaching on contraception and sterilization or are actually involved in it. Is it no wonder that so few go to confession and lead a deep prayer life.

2. Married life—This can be seen in the scandalous fifty-percent divorce rate among Catholics and most knowledgeable commentators attribute this to the contraceptive mentality. It effects women more than men because of their God given sensitive nature. It only stands to reason that if a women has to sacrifice her personhood and is forced to become a thing or an object of pleasure, and to be available whenever she's needed, a coldness sets in, which often times leads to divorce and the inevitable permanent scars left on the couple and their children.

3. Vocations—the average age of the priest in the United States is approximately sixty-three years. Today in our country Bishops are presiding over priestly burial societies. Churches are closing or being consolidated. Let's face it, religious have practically disappeared from our schools and hospitals. This is self-evident. Vocations, seldom, if ever, come from contracepting families. Contraception is selfish and a this-worldly mentality. This syndrome does not breed the generous children who will give themselves to the priesthood or the consecrated life.

This is not a condemnation of you, my dear parishioners. Many have never heard this message proclaimed. Many too have received conflicting advice from those who should have known better. If we speak about blame, perhaps a large part of it must be shouldered by us clergy who have been delinquent in preaching about this matter and following through with good Natural Family Planning.

But this is not the time to criticize. We've had enough of this. Let us remember that God is merciful, and that He will forgive any sin if we are really sorry. Go to confession, ask God's pardon and live according to His teachings. Thank God for the Sacrament of conversion (Confession). For those of you who find this teaching difficult to accept, do not just say I've made up my mind and I just disagree with the Church! Please remember that Christ and the Church are one and that when you disagree with the Church, you disagree with Jesus Christ and you condemn yourself. It is in the Church through Baptism that you are made a child of God; it is in the Church that you are Confirmed in the Holy Spirit; it is in the Church that you are forgiven; it is in the Church that you eat the Body and drink the Blood of the Lord (could you have a more personal relationship than this?); it is in the Church that you are prepared to meet your Maker at the end of life in the Sacrament of Annointing; you are married in the Church, and you are made a priest in the Church. How can one disagree with the Church and still call themselves a Catholic? Instead, go to Our Lord humbly on your knees and ask Him to open up your hard heart and dull mind. I can almost assure you that within seconds He will perform this miracle.

Just a quick note to Physicians: I know that many of you work very hard in your professions and are looked up to by society. The Lord wants you to be a beacon of light for your patients in these matters of life. You might say, that I have no right to force my Catholic teachings upon my patients. But let me say to you, that your patients have no right to force their immorality on you! One day you will stand before your judge. This advice is applicable to all health care professionals.

In closing: to our young people—all of you want a happy marriage; you are sick and tired of divorce and the evil it has brought on you and upon the world. If you want God's blessings upon your future marriage, I beg of you not to allow the poisonous venom of contraception and sterilization to enter into it. If you stay away from these, God will give your marriage His choicest blessings.

(Private)—I am available to discuss these matters with you privately at your convenience. Please do not hesitate to take me up on this offer as I love you very much.

May Our Blessed Lady grant to us clergy and to you her precious gift of chastity. AMEN

Father Tom Knoblach
Church of St. Joseph, Bertha, Minnesota
Church of St. Edward, Henning, Minnesota

The story is told of a monk many years ago who came to the abbot of his community and confessed that he had been guilty of gossip about a brother monk. The abbot listened patiently, and then told him, "For your penance, I want you to take a feather pillow, go to the center of town square, and then tear open the pillow and scatter the feathers to the wind. Then come back to see me."

The monk thought it a strange penance, but in obedience, he did so.

When he returned, the abbot asked him, "Did you do as I asked?"

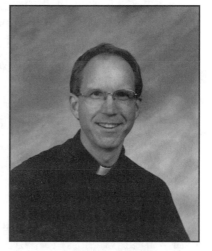

Father Thomas Knoblach
Consultant for health-care ethics and pastor of two parishes, Diocese of St. Cloud, Minnesota

"Yes, Father Abbot," the monk replied.

"Good," the abbot said. "Now, I want you to go back to the town square and gather up all the feathers again."

"But," the monk protested, "that would be impossible! They are all over the countryside!"

"Then you understand," the abbot replied, "what damage happens with gossip."

You may well wonder what the monk's feathers have to do with Natural Family Planning and contraception. One of the central insights of our Christian faith is the notion of the common good . . . that we are not isolated individuals alone in the world, but called to live and thrive in community. We are persons created in the image of the Triune God, Who is love—Father, Son, and Spirit. We find our fulfillment as persons in love, in mutual relationships of giving and receiving. Humans are created for relationship . . . that is why solitary confinement is considered a severe punishment, why cults isolate their members from family to manipulate them, why loneliness gives all of us blue days once in a while.

This idea of solidarity or community is in rather stark contrast to our culture, with its stress on radical individualism. To completely describe the origins and effects of this individualism would take far too long, but the phenomenon is pretty well known to all of us. Radical doubts about religious authority, about claims to revealed truth, about anything stable and certain except the claims of science, have filtered down to sitcoms and pop music and public commentary. Where no one seems to know much for sure, it becomes easy for everyone to decide for oneself about what is true, what is right, what is worth striving for. In much simpler terms: the mottos for the age become, "Look out for Number One. Take care of yourself. Go for the gusto. Just do it. All we have is now."

Couples who choose contraception usually go through some thought process to make their decision. Sometimes, their reasons are basically selfish, they simply don't want to be burdened with the costs and bother of children right now. But that may in fact reflect a truth . . . if they are really that self-centered, then perhaps they indeed are not ready for children. Often enough, though, I believe, they have reasons that *Humanae Vitae* might support: serious concerns about health, or family economics, or their capacity to care for one more child in the family network. As Paul VI noted, though, even such good intentions do not justify any means to achieve them. The means used must also pass ethical muster. And that is where abortion, sterilization, or mechanical and chemical forms of contraception all fail: they violate the intrinsic, God-given meaning of human sexuality and conjugal love by intentionally acting to frustrate that meaning. The sexual embrace achieves its full meaning only when it is a true exchange that is open to love and to life . . . when it is a total gift of self to one's spouse through the body—just as Christ unites Himself with us in the Eucharist, giving us both love and new life through His Body and Blood. Abortion, sterilization, and contraception —and, in fact things, like *in vitro* fertilization and human cloning—all act to sunder these meanings. They select one aspect by eliminating the other.

When a couple chooses NFP and openness to life, they not only serve God's will but also their own sanctification and their family. They not only serve the human community directly through blessing it with children, who are in fact in increasingly short supply in the developed world, where most countries are just at or even below replacement levels, thanks to abortion and contraception. They also make a sacrifice for the common good in a way that is more indirect, but perhaps even more important. They create a trend . . . they create precisely what John Paul II calls for in *Evangelium Vitae*—a new culture of life. Let me explain.

Lee Silver is a molecular biologist at Yale who wrote a book a few years back called *Remaking Eden*. The book is mostly about cloning and test-tube babies and genetic engineering . . . all the new ways of making babies that substitute technological interventions for the good old-fashioned way. Silver argues that there is no master plan or conspiracy that has ushered in this new era in reproduction . . . it is just that couples, one by one, for their own reasons and considering their own situation, make a choice. And when you have enough couples doing that, you achieve a kind of critical mass that creates a social trend . . . a new culture.

That explains what has happened in the last forty years or so in our Western contraceptive culture . . . as I said earlier, individual couples making their own choice based on their own needs and situation, but without consideration of the larger community they were affecting by that choice. That effect is not just direct—they have less children—but it also contributes to the strengthening of the ideas that individual decisions can be made in isolation, that one need not consider their effect on the larger whole, that having children is solely a private enterprise in which God and the community have no input and no interest. But Paul VI saw married couples as stewards, not masters, of the creation of new life; they were to be allies, not adversaries, of the Church's mission in their vocation.

When a couple chooses how to space the birth of their children, they simply cannot do so in isolation, for they are embedded in a network of relationships and in a society. They will either contribute to the growth of the culture they live in, or its decline—there is no neutral territory, no fence to sit on. They either side with the contraceptive culture, or they contribute to the new culture of life.

No one set out with a master plan to undermine respect for life on such a broad scale . . . it is simply the accumulation of a vast number of individual choices. And the antidote works the same way . . . the culture will change when there is a greater number, a critical mass, of individual choices for life. Every couple is essential in this struggle . . . each decision that we make weighs on one side of the scale or the other, and tips the balance. We are the light to the nations; we are chosen by Christ in this age, precisely for this work. In their daily living and their love open to life, couples who choose NFP are invaluable agents in this new culture of life.

Father Anthony Oelrich
Diocese of St. Cloud, Minnesota

What a wonderful witness to hope! Whenever two people declare their desire to publicly give their lives to each other, a remarkable faith is revealed. They are saying, "We truly believe that the love we share is deep enough and strong enough to last a lifetime!"

Father Anthony Oelrich
Priest of the Diocese of St. Cloud,
Minnesota, studying in Rome, Italy.

What makes this so amazing is that such boldness exists in the context of a society such as ours, where so many of us, indeed all of us, have been touched by failed love, broken promises and shattered dreams. In the midst of profound encounters with human beings' inability to keep lifetime commitments, so many continue to live out of the conviction, when professing their marriage vows, that love for a lifetime is possible and real!

This highlights the tension which those who are planning for marriage, and those who are married, live with. Within them are conflicting witnesses. The experience of love they have found in their relationship speaks to them of something for a lifetime. So many experiences they have had in life speak of the painful reality that such relationships often simply do not make it. I find many young people, struggling with this tension, finding the call to a lifetime commitment a fearful and perhaps impossible dream. Relationships can be difficult! The perma-

116

nent nature of marriage raises serious questions: "Can I keep a promise over a lifetime?" "Can I trust the promise of this other for a lifetime?" "Are such commitments even realistic in our day and age?"

It is with a deep sense of this very real challenge that I want to place before the married and those preparing for marriage the beautiful and wonderful teaching of our Lord Jesus concerning our human sexuality. Concretely, I want to invite you to view your sexuality through the lens of Natural Family Planning (NFP). I am absolutely convinced that we live in gifted days. I sense very much that Jesus, by the gentle action of his Holy Spirit is guiding his Church into a deeper and more wonderful understanding of the vocation of marriage. I am convinced even further that NFP is a gift, or you might say a discipline, that helps safeguard and protect the commitment of love for a lifetime. I am grateful for this opportunity to share with you what I believe is a very precious gift, the Church's teaching on contraception and NFP.

In the home I grew up in with my family, my mother had a hutch. The hutch was a beautiful cabinet with glass doors. As beautiful as the cabinet was, the real beauty was within, for it was in the hutch that my mother stored her most precious dinnerware and glassware. All of us as kids learned early on to move gently around that hutch. What was inside was not only precious but delicate. What is precious and delicate, that hutch taught me, needs to be treated with great care, given its own special space.

I often think of my mother's hutch when I reflect on relationships, especially the relationship of marriage. What can possibly be of greater value, more precious and dear than the one a person entrusts him or herself to for life? What, also, can be more delicate? Our modern age has taught us this, certainly: relationships can indeed be very fragile realities. Marriage relationships, precious and delicate, need to be treated with care and given special space. This, I believe, is one of the great gifts of NFP! It is a very concrete way of building care and that special space into the marriage relationship.

Let me, to begin, speak directly to you about what NFP is. NFP *is a modern, scientific and natural means of either avoiding or achieving pregnancy. It requires no drugs, devices, or operations of any kind. World Health Organization studies (and other national and international studies) conclude the Billings Ovulation Method has an average use-effectiveness of 99.15 percent in avoiding pregnancy when couples are properly taught and the method is correctly followed. With proper instruction and follow-up, couples are able to recognize days of infertility and potential fertility in each cycle*

Those are the basic facts concerning NFP. What I want to share is the deeper, and much more valuable, reality that NFP opens up to a married couple. I want to make this so very clear: the Church sees our sexuality as an awesome gift of God! As a matter of fact, the Church views the sexual embrace of a husband and wife as a powerful 'sacramental' window through which we human beings come to see the truth about God.

You see, Jesus revealed to us that God is not simply some great, eternal, almighty, isolated being out there somewhere far away from anyone or anything else. No! God is, from all eternity, a family. A relationship of being. Father, Son, and Holy Spirit. The very foundation of all reality, God, is this eternal relationship of love that is so total, so complete that three persons are in fact one God.

Within all of human experience, where is this most beautifully displayed before us? In the sexual embrace of a husband and wife, where total, permanent, and fruitful love is given bodily expression. Two become one, open to another flowing from their loving embrace.

NFP safeguards this most sacred, awesome act of the husband and wife. It does so because it calls the couple to be attentive to their bodies. Where contraception can mask fertility of the body, and, therefore, mask the other in some sense, NFP calls the husband to be attentive to the fertility of his wife, and, therefore, attentive to her person. NFP, as a matter of fact, demands the attention of both wife and husband in order to succeed. Fertility cannot become the responsibility of just one of them. It promotes and calls forth shared responsibility and, therefore, will be open new paths of communication.

Shared responsibility. New paths of communication. NFP will also be an on-going reminder to honor one another and to never take the other for granted. The seven to ten days of abstinence (if pregnancy is to be avoided for some necessary reason) is a built-in safeguard against taking one another for granted. How devastating it is to marriages when one feels like they are being "used." The periodic abstinence in NFP will call husbands and wives to find ways of expressing their love other than sexual intercourse. Again, NFP encourages communication. It nurtures a holistic and holy love between spouses.

There are so many other things that could be said about the Church's understanding of marriage and, in particular, sexuality. I wanted, however, to make the special invitation to all who are discerning the vocation to marriage. There are so many fears connected to the lifetime commitment marriage entails. The Church, I so strongly believe, offers the best, good news to safeguard and make possible that wonderful commitment. Natural Family Planning is one of the most precious, and beautiful supports the Church has to offer couples who long to know the peace, the joy, and the fulfillment of life-long marriage.

On the Connection between Contraception and Abortion
Fr. Augustine H.T. Tran, Archdiocese of Atlanta, GA

We come now to the end of October, and, hence, to the end of our series on life issues. The final topic that I should like to discuss is one that is rarely associated with the issue of respecting human life, at least outside of Catholic theology. The issue is that of artificial birth control.

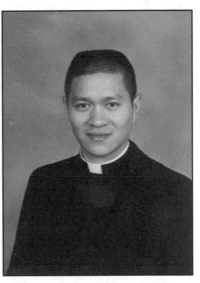

Father Augustine Tran
Priest of the Archdiocese of Atlanta, Georgia

As Catholics and as Christians, we are not called to be anti-abortion. We are called to be pro-life, and one cannot be pro-life and pro-contraception. Contraception is contra-conception, against-conception. Against the conception of what? Well, against the conception of life. Hence, it makes no logical sense that one would be pro-life and yet against the conception of life.

The issues of abortion and contraception are two branches of the same tree. The most obvious connection in this regard is to look at those contraceptives that, in actuality, act as abortifacients: the IUD, oral contraceptives such as the progestin-only and estrogen-progestin pills, injectable contraceptives such as Depo-Provera, and contraceptive implants such as Norplant. When we read the medical literature on these so-called contraceptives, we see that they do not always prevent conception, but rather kill the conceptus. They prevent that which has already been conceived, the person who has already been conceived, from implanting on the uterine wall. Hence, they work, perhaps not all of the time, perhaps not even most of the time, but at least some of the time, by aborting a person who has already been conceived by hindering him from implanting on the uterine wall, completely unbeknownst to the woman using them. If we truly believe that human life is sacred, then every human life is sacred, and it is sacred from conception to natural death, therefore, killing even one innocent person by this method would be unacceptable. Hence, all of those so-called contraceptives that can and do work as an abortifacient must be rejected by the pro-life position.

During the confirmation hearings for our current attorney general, John Ashcroft, he was called an extremist for holding this position, which is completely consistent, not just with Catholic theology, but also with medical fact. Somehow, it's extreme to have a logically consistent point of view.

This is, of course, only the most obvious connection between contraception and abortion; what about those contraceptives that do not act as abortifacients? How do we disrespect human life by using them? Here, we can see perhaps not an intrinsic connection, but the moral momentum that leads us from one to the other.

My moral theology professor used to say that once we are willing to do violence to an act, then it is only a baby step until we are willing to do violence to the product of that act. To understand what he meant, we have to look at the conjugal act and understand God's design for that act.

But first, why am I talking about the conjugal act, the marital act, and not just the sexual act? It would seem obvious that all talk of the morality of contraception must take place within the context of marriage. Since all carnal knowledge outside the marital covenant is already illicit, it makes very little sense to talk about contraception in that context. Nevertheless, the most common argument used in that context is to say that our kids are going to have sex anyway, so we had better give them some protection.

But what sane man would say, "Well, the Nazis are going to kill all the Jews, anyway, so let's just help them find painless, humane ways of doing it?" Or what loving father would say, "Well, my son is going to rob that bank, anyway, so let me buy him a bullet-proof vest so he won't get killed in the process?" So why, then, would anyone say, "Well, my daughter's going to have sex, anyway, so I'd better get her on the pill and buy her some condoms so she won't get pregnant or sick?" They all follow the same line of faulty reasoning. Obviously, then, we have to confine our discussion to within the context of the marital covenant. Outside of the marital covenant, we need to be talking about something completely different, which is not to say that fornication and contraception are not related, because they are. They both attack the sanctity of marriage, but how they do that is different . . . related, but different.

Now, as I eluded to earlier, the Church's teachings on contraception have very little to do with birth control and everything to do with preserving the sanctity of marriage. Every papal encyclical that has addressed this issue is an encyclical not on the morality of contraception, but on the sanctity of the marriage covenant. It is because the Church wishes to be faithful to her Lord and to preserve the sanctity of marriage that she continues to defend the biblical and traditional condemnation of artificial birth control . . . not because it is artificial, but because it is unnatural. This is a very important distinction. Artificial forms of birth control are evil, not because they are artificial, but because they are unnatural, because they frustrate the natural ends of the conjugal act as God has designed it, those ends that unite man with God in the unitive and procreative aspects of conjugal love.

To understand what we mean by natural ends, consider the act of eating. What is the natural end of the act of eating? It is not to eat what we like. It is not to enjoy the company of friends. The natural end of eating is nourishment. It is good to eat the foods that we like so that we might enjoy eating; and it is good to eat with friends so that we might enjoy fellowship. But if we are stranded on an island without friends and without any food that we like, do we stop eating? No! We still eat whatever we can to stay alive no matter what it tastes like.

So, what do we call it when we willfully, deliberately frustrate this natural end of eating, when we willfully choose to stop the food from nourishing our bodies? What do we call bulimia and anorexia? We call them eating disorders!

Well, so, too, is the conjugal act disordered when we willfully frustrate the natural ends for which God designed it, when love and life (or more technically, union and procreation) are willfully divided or frustrated, which is precisely what a contraceptive does.

This is what my professor called doing violence to an act. By frustrating God's design, by not allowing an act to do what it is designed to do, we are doing violence to that act. Once we've done violence to that act, then we very easily move to doing violence to the product of that act, which is what abortion is, doing violence to the life that is created by the conjugal act.

We need only look at the history of Planned Parenthood to see how this works itself out in the real world. Planned Parenthood began with the sole purpose of providing easy access to artificial contraceptives. This was in the 1910s. In less than a century, it has become the number one provider of surgical abortions in the world.

Our own U.S. Supreme Court made this connection between contraception and abortion explicit when, in 1992, in *Planned Parenthood v. Casey*, the Court said, "It should be recognized, moreover, that in some critical respects, the abortion decision is of the same character as the decision to use contraception, to which *Griswold v. Connecticut, Eisenstadt v. Baird*, and *Carey v. Population Services International* afford constitutional protection." The Court went on to say that "abortion is customarily chosen as an unplanned response to the consequence of unplanned activity or to the failure of conventional birth control." The Court here recognized that the vast majority of abortions are performed as just another form of contraception: "Oops, my contraceptive failed; I'd better get an abortion." Once we are willing to do violence to an act, it's only a baby step until we are willing to do violence to the product of that act.

In fact, *Roe v. Wade* was decided based upon the constitutional right of privacy. Well, the right of privacy was first established by the Court in 1965 in *Griswold v. Connecticut*, which was the case that legalized the sale of contraceptives in the state of Connecticut. It was in that case that dissenting Justice Stewart wrote, "I can find no such general right of privacy in the Bill of Rights, in any other part of the Constitution, or in any case ever before decided by this Court." Both the dissenting justices in that case recognized the right to certain privacies in our Constitution, but no overarching "right of privacy." That "right of privacy" was then used as the basis for legalizing the murder of innocent babies in the womb in 1973.

The point of this discussion is merely to demonstrate that contraception is not just a method but also a mentality. It is a whole way of viewing love, life, and the conjugal act, the act that God designed to join those two realities. This is the moral momentum that connects them together. The history of this nation's laws demonstrates how intimately connected they are. There is no way to reverse the culture of death, to increase our respect for the dignity of human life throughout the world, without first learning to respect the sanctity of the act that creates that life.

Respecting the conjugal act not only leads to a respect for the life of the unborn, but also for the life of the spouses that are engaged in that act. The conjugal act is an act of total self-donation: "I give myself fully to you, and I accept you fully." Spouses are repeating with their bodies what they said on their wedding day with their lips: "for better, for worse, for richer, for poorer, in sickness and in health until death do us part." That is total self-donation and total acceptance of another for life. In a contraceptive act, we now no longer give ourselves to the other fully, nor do we accept the other fully: "I give you all of me except my reproductive self"; "I accept all of you except your reproductive self." Once the conjugal act stops being total self-donation, it quickly becomes selfish. It is no longer about what I give to you, but about what I get from you.

Selfishness is the first step in destroying relationships, in destroying our relationship with God and in destroying relationships with our neighbors. It is well-known that the majority of Catholics in this country reject the Church's teaching on contraception, a teaching that the Church has consistently held for 2,000 years and which every Christian Church held until 1930. A teaching that the Church intimately connects with preserving the sanctity of marriage because, of course, marriage and the marital act are intimately connected, inseparable, in fact. If we do violence to the marital act, not only shall we be led to doing violence to the product of that act, but we shall also be doing violence to marriage itself. It is also well-known that the Catholic divorce rate is essentially the same as the national divorce rate, which is fifty percent; what is less well known is that the divorce rate of those who practice natural methods of family planning, methods that respect the conjugal act and its procreative as well as its unitive aspects, is less than two percent.

So, finally, the question is asked, why does each conjugal act have to be open to life? Can't a marriage be open to life as a whole without each conjugal act being open to life?

Well, why does each conjugal act have to be with my wife? Can't I be faithful to my marriage as a whole without each marital act having to be with my wife? I mean, isn't ninety-nine percent of the time sufficient to make me faithful to my marriage as a whole? Well, obviously, no! And so it is with the covenant of love and life. Just as respecting human life means respecting every human life from conception to natural death, so, also, being open to human life means being open with every conjugal act. And according to God's design, openness to life means openness to love, which are both necessary to have happy and holy marriages.

Scriptural Opportunities

Introduction

The following are examples of Scriptural texts appearing in the course of the three-year Sunday cycle of readings that can be used as "launching pads" to speak on NFP and related issues. For some of the passages, I have indicated some brief idea of the connection I have in mind.

This list, of course, is not intended to be exhaustive but merely illustrative of the options available through the liturgical calendar. As you look through, you will readily see other texts not listed here.

I do not believe it is prudent to repeat this message at every possible opportunity mentioned below, lest it become nagging and annoying to people and other important themes go unaddressed. Your openness to the Holy Spirit will lead you to the best ways to present this preachable message.

(Note: the texts quoted are from the New American Bible. Different translations will of course have slightly different wording but the major themes remain the same.)

Father Tom Knoblach

Advent

In general, this can be preached as a season of conversion and to "prepare the way of the Lord." The use of NFP rather than contraception can be a part of this message of conversion.

Examples of texts in particular:

I Advent A—Is. 2: 1-5: ". . . that he may instruct us in his ways and we may walk in his paths . . . come, let us walk in the light of the Lord."

Rom 13:11-14: "Let us cast off deeds of darkness and put on the armor of light."

I Advent B—Is 63:16-19; 64:2-7: "Why do you let us wander, O Lord, from your ways, and harden our hearts so that we fear you not?"

I Advent C—I Thes 3:12-4:2: "even as you learned from us how to conduct yourselves in a way pleasing to God—which you are indeed doing—so you must learn to make still greater progress."

II Advent A. B. and C—all of these readings quote John the Baptist quoting Isaiah: "Prepare the way of the Lord, make straight his paths." A connection might be drawn to preparing the way of the Lord who gives life in married love.

III Advent A—James 5:7-10: "Be patient until the coming of the Lord . . . steady your hearts . . ."—the patience of periodic abstinence as an expression of this deeper patience of waiting upon God's plan.

Mt 11:2-11: "The least-born into the Kingdom of God is greater than [John]"—an opportunity to address the greatness of Christian parenthood.

III Advent B—I Thes 5:16-24: "Do not stifle the spirit . . . avoid any semblance of evil. . . . May you be preserved whole and entire, spirit, soul, and body . . ."—about the integrity and wholeness of married love via NFP.

III Advent C—Phil 4:4-7—"Everyone should see how unselfish you are"—the witness of openness to life and a large family as a visible testimony to the unselfishness of love.

IV Advent A—Mt 1:18-24: "It is by the Holy Spirit that she has conceived this child"—true of every conception, accepting life as a gift from God.

IV Advent B—Lk 1:26-38: "Let it be done to me according to your word."

IV Advent C—Lk 1:39-45: "Blessed is she who trusted that the Lord's words to her would be fulfilled."

Holy Family—obvious time to speak about the sublime vocation of parenthood and family.

Mary, Mother of God—opportunity to speak of dignity of motherhood and Mary's example of trust and obedient faith, that can be imitated by every mother and father.

Epiphany—the Wise follow the Light of heavenly guidance on their Journey of faith, to find the Truth and offer their most precious gifts—the analogies are obvious for married love.

Lent

Lent is the great season of conversion and repentance as we strive to be purified to die and rise with Christ anew in the great Easter sacramental mysteries. Another opportunity to call people to deeper conversion and witness to holiness of life.

133

I Lent A—Gen 2:7-9, 3:1-7—the Temptation and Fall—obvious implications for contemporary temptations to create our own moral order; contrast with Christ's fidelity in Mt 4:1-11; can be done with B and C as well.

II Lent A—Gen 12:1-4—the trust of Abram and the promised blessing of children.

II Lent A. B. C—the Gospels of the Transfiguration present the invitation to "Listen" to the beloved Son of God as He speaks through His Church.

III Lent A—Jn 4:5-42—the Woman at the Well provides a beautiful illustration of the way Jesus works with us gently, firmly, and *gradually* to lead us to the truth and make us evangelizers.

III Lent B—Ex 20:1-17—the Commandments are an obvious opportunity; in Jn 2:13-25, Jesus is "well aware of what is in man's heart"—Christ understands our struggles and will help us.

III Lent C—Lk 13:1-9—again the notion of the Lord's patience and gradual call to conversion, which remains necessary for us.

IV Lent A—I Sm 16:1-13—"Not as man sees does God see . . . the Lord looks into the heart"—the value of trusting not in our own understandings but on God's word and wisdom; reinforce with Jn 9:1-41 about vision and blindness (in our lives and in our culture).

IV Lent B—all the readings speak of the Lord's mercy, the motive and reassurance of conversion.

IV Lent C—Lk 15:1-32—the Prodigal Son is the classic story of conversion, "coming to his senses at last."

V Lent A—raising of Lazarus is assurance of renewal of our lives by the same power of Christ.

V Lent B—Jer 31:31-34—"I will place my law within them, and write it on their hearts"—the gift of a rightly formed conscience.

V Lent C—Jn 8:1-11: "Nor do I condemn you . . . from now on, avoid this sin—the assurance of forgiveness and the need to change our lives.

Easter Season

Any of the Easter season texts can be used to illustrate the joy of living according to the New Way of Christ, the victor over sin and the Lord of Life, who remains with us until the end of time. Also important is the growth of the Church, which continues to speak the saving truth of Christ through the Holy Spirit. For example:

III Easter C—Acts 5:27-41: "Better for us to obey God than men."

IV Easter A—Acts 2:14, 36-41: "Save yourself from this generation that has gone astray."

I Pt 2:20-25: "If you put up with suffering for doing what is right, this is acceptable in God's eyes."

Jn 10:1-10: "I came that they might have life, and have it to the full."

V Easter A—I Pt 2:4-9—the stone rejected by the builders as the cornerstone—many reject teaching of *Humanae Vitae* but it is cornerstone of family and society.

V Easter B—Jn 15:1-8: "He prunes away every barren branch, but the fruitful ones he trims clean to increase their yield"—sacrifice is necessary to be fruitful for the Lord.

V Easter C—Acts 14:21-27: "We must undergo many trials if we are to enter the reign of God."

Rv 21:1-5: "See, I make all things new!"—Christ renews married love.

Jn 14:15-21—the Paraclete comes to those who obey Christ's commandments.

VI Easter B—readings speak of God's love made manifest in Christ—reflect on the nature of authentic love sacramentalized in marriage, creative of ever-deeper personal union and of new life; Jesus' words, "I call you friends," emphasizes the role of spouses as free and conscious co-workers with Christ in the new civilization of love.

VI Easter C—Acts 15:22-29—the explicit mention of "illicit sexual union" is an opening.

Ordinary Time

The focus of Ordinary Time is the teaching, miracles, and ministry of Jesus, and bringing these mysteries into our daily lives.

2nd Sunday A—Is 49:3-6—the vocation of each from the womb, the dignity of every human life (see also 4th Sunday C, Jer 1:4-5).

2nd Sunday B—1 Sm 3:3-1 0—"Speak, Lord, your servant is listening"—openness to the voice of the Lord under the guidance of the Church.

I Cor 6:13-20—"The body is not for immorality, it is for the Lord . . . glorify God in your body."

2nd Sunday C—Jn 2:1-12—the wedding at Cana is an opportunity to speak about the dignity of marriage; the wine running out can be a symbol of the emptiness of human life without the grace of Jesus; "only the servants knew" implies that those who serve at the word of Christ are in on the "secret" of the sources of new life in the Gospel message.

3rd Sunday A, B, and C—all are calls to "reform your lives, the Kingdom is at hand."

4th Sunday A—Mt 5:1-12—the assurance in the Beatitudes that the sacrifices of today will have their reward; see also 6th Sunday C, Lk 6:20-26.

4th Sunday C—I Cor 12:31-13:13—the characteristics of true love.

5th Sunday A—Mt 5:13-16: "You are the light of the world . . . you are the salt of the earth"—if the faithful do not witness to the New Way, who will? (See also 5th Sunday C, Is 6:8: "Here I am, send me!")

6th Sunday A—Sir 15:15-20: "If you choose you can keep the commandments . . ."—the freedom and responsibility of the human will.

I Cor 2:6-10—the wisdom of the spiritually mature, mysterious and hidden.

7th Sunday A—Lv 19:1-2: "Be holy, for I, the Lord, your God, am holy."

I Cor 3.16-23. "For the temple of God is holy, and you are that temple . . . the wisdom of this world is absurdity with God."

7th Sunday C—Lk 6:27-38: "The measure you measure with will be measured back to you"—openness to God's wisdom and to life will impact our future, especially as we age and become dependent on others for care.

8th Sunday A—Is 49:14-15—the Lord's faithful love illustrated by mother's love for infant.

Mt 6:24-34—trust in God's providence rather than human calculation; present idea of responsible parenthood from *Humanae Vitae.*

8th Sunday B—Mk 2:18-22: "New wine is poured into new skins"—the need for renewal of mind to follow Christ, rather than trying to combine the ways of the world and the ways of the Gospel.

9th Sunday A—Mt 7:21-2—need to put the Lord's words into practice; need not merely to know but to live the truth.

9th Sunday B—II Cor 4:6-11—we possess the treasure of God's truth and our power to create new life in earthen vessels; this power comes from God, not from us; thus we can endure the hardships it entails.

10th Sunday A—Gen 3:9-15—Abraham's faith rewarded with children; the call to follow the Lord even as sinful people, that we might be healed and changed.

11th Sunday A—Mt 9:36-10:8—the call of the Apostles reminds us that we are also all called by Christ; the gift couples have received—their fertility—they are to give as a gift.

11th Sunday B—Mk 4:26-34—faith (in the wisdom of God's plan) the size of the mustard seed bears great results.

12th Sunday B—Mk 4:35-41—Jesus calming the storm reassures us that He will also care for married couples who are open to life.

12th Sunday C—Lk 9:18-24: "Whoever loses his life for my sake will save it"—the assurance of reward for sacrifice.

13th Sunday A—II Kgs 4:8-16—the woman of Shumen is rewarded for welcoming God's messenger Elisha with a child.

Mt 10:37-42: "He who welcomes you welcomes me"—accepting children welcomes Christ.

13th Sunday C—Gal 5:1, 13-18: "Do not take on yourselves the yoke of slavery . . . you have been called to live in freedom"—the freedom of conscience and life that NFP brings, refusing the slavery of contemporary culture.

14th Sunday A—Mt 11:25-30: "What you have hidden from the learned and the clever you have revealed to the merest children"—the dignity of children and the transcendent wisdom of God's plan that does not make sense in merely human terms.

14th Sunday B—Mk 6.1-6. "He could work no miracles there because of their lack of faith"—in resisting God's plan via contraception, the Spirit can work no miracles of transformation and new life in our lives.

15th Sunday A—Is 55:10-11—the Word of God never fails in its purpose; we can trust His wisdom reflected in NFP.

Rom 8: 18-23—we groan inwardly while we await the full revelation of God's wisdom Mt 13:1-23—openness to God's Word brings a rich harvest. . . .

15th Sunday C-Dt 30:10-14: "[God's commandment] is something very near to you . . . you have only to carry it out"—the power and freedom of the will to live NFP.

16th Sunday A—Mt 13:24-43—parables of weeds in the wheat (need to learn to live with suffering and adversity and sacrifice; NFP's chosen sacrifices bring spiritual strength and maturity); mustard seed and leaven (small acts of faith yield great results).

16th Sunday C—Gen 18:1-10—Abraham's hospitality to the three strangers is rewarded with a child in fidelity to the covenant promises of God; can be reinforced with the "better portion" of Mary in the Gospel (Lk 10:38-42).

17th Sunday A—I Kgs 3:5-12—Solomon's prayer for wisdom invites us to pray like him to know what is right and wrong and live accordinfgly; Rom 8:28-30 reassures us that when we strive to live this way, God will make all things work together for the good; Mt 13:44-52 suggests that NFP can help us find the pearl of great price in married life (fidelity, communication, peace, children).

17th Sunday B—Jn 6:1-15: ". . . but what good is that for so many?"—an invitation to overcome our fears about limited resources by entrusting them to the hands of Christ, where they become more than enough.

17th Sunday C—Lk 11:1-13: "Ask and you shall receive . . ." —this famous passage assures us that God will answer our prayers for patience, strength, fidelity, self-mastery.

18th Sunday B—Ex 16:2-15—the story of the quail and the manna assures us that God will provide when we call upon Him in faith and strive to follow His ways.

Eph 4:17-24: "Lay aside . . . the old self which deteriorates through illusion and desire"—a very rich passage implying that life without accepting God's grace causes us to come apart through illusion (falsehoods perceived as truth) and desire (disordered inclinations).

18th Sunday C—Col 3:1-11—a clear invitation to put to death whatever in our nature is rooted in earth, among which contraception and sterilization can easily be examples.

Lk 12:13-21: "A man may be wealthy, but his possessions do not guarantee him life"—the primacy of persons over things; the poverty of material wealth with no heirs. . . .

19th Sunday A—I Kgs 19:9-13—Elijah encounters God in the tiny whispering sound, implying that God's voice is often drowned out by modern materialistic and contraceptive culture, so we need to listen and wait carefully to hear him.

19th Sunday C—Wis 18:6-9: "For in secret the holy children of the good were offering sacrifice and putting into effect with one accord the divine institution"—while this refers to the Passover meal, it is an evocative image of a "conspiracy of goodness" that NFP couples enact by offering the sacrifices it entails and putting God's saving will into effect, as individual couples but united in following the same divine directive. This active faith is affirmed in Heb 11:1-12 and in Lk 12:32-48, where Jesus counsels renunciation and trust in divine providence.

20th Sunday C—Heb 12:1-4—the perseverance of Jesus inspires our sacrifices and encourages us not to abandon the holy struggle of faith and obedience to God's will. Lk 12:49-53 speaks of the division that can result even in families over Christ and his teaching, but calls us to choose the way of the Lord.

21st Sunday A—Rom 11:33-36 acknowledges the inscrutable ways of the Lord, which often contradict merely human wisdom (as in the appropriate openness to life in married love); Mt 16:13-20 reminds us that the Church's voice is that of Christ, who has bound potential fertility to intercourse.

21st Sunday B—Eph 5:21-32—the classic text for expounding on the characteristics of Christian married love as an image of Christ and His Church; Christ's love comes to us in the union of persons that takes place through the Body in the Eucharist, and is always open to the transmission of the new life of grace. Jn 6:60-69, although about the Eucharist, presents the basic choice we all face before the Lord: "Do you want to leave me, too?" Couples using NFP choose to stay with Christ and His wisdom.

22nd Sunday A—Rom 12:1-2—Paul's appeal to be transformed by the renewal of our minds, and not conformed to the ideas of the present (contraceptive) age, so that we may accurately judge God's perfect will. Mt 16:21-27 reinforces this idea of judging by God's standards, not by man's.

22nd Sunday B—Dt 4:1-8—obedience to God's commandments gives evidence of our wisdom to others (one can make the demographic arguments in favor of openness to life given our shrinking Western population)—one cannot be a "great nation" without children.

23rd Sunday B—James 2:1-5: "Did not God choose those who are poor in the eyes of the world to be rich in faith and heirs of the kingdom . . .?"—large families are often materially less wealthy, but have far greater riches in faith and love.

24th Sunday A—Rom 14:7-9—spouses are not masters of the powers of life and fertility, but servants of the Lord, as *Humanae Vitae* also teaches.

24th Sunday B—James 2:14-18: ". . . I will show you the faith that underlies my works"—openness to life gives visible witness to faith in the birth of children; Mk 8:27-35 again invites us to judge by divine and not human standards.

24th Sunday C—Lk 15:1-32—the Prodigal Son story is the perfect text to invite conversion and assurance of a new beginning in God's mercy, coming to our senses at last.

25th Sunday A—Is 55:6-9 reaffirms the truth that God's ways are not human ways; we can trust in God's superior wisdom in NFP; the parable of Mt 20: 1-16 assures us that no matter how long we have resisted this wisdom, we can still change and be welcomed by the Lord.

25th Sunday B—Wis 2:12-20—NFP couples often face the persecution prophesied here, but can have the same confidence of Jesus that God will take care of them; James 3:16-4:3 speaks of the wisdom from above that these couples have accepted; Jesus' words in Mk 9:30-37 clearly teach the surpassing value of welcoming children for his sake.

27th Sunday B—Mk 10:2-16: "Let the children come to me and do not hinder them. It is to just such as these that the Kingdom of God belongs. . . ."

28th Sunday B—Mk 10:17-30—the danger of riches; couples open to large families are spared this selfishness and use the things of this world for the noblest purpose. . . .

Trinity Sunday A, B, and C—the self-giving love that is God is mirrored in married love. . . .